# Southern
# Belle
## To
# Hollywood
## Hell

# Southern Belle To Hollywood Hell

## CORLISS PALMER AND HER SCANDALOUS RISE AND FALL

### BY JENNIFER ANN REDMOND

BearManor Media

2018

*Southern Belle To Hollywood Hell:*
*Corliss Palmer and Her Scandalous Rise and Fall*

© 2018  Jennifer Ann Redmond

Published in the United States of America by:

Bear Manor Media
P. O. Box 71426
Albany, GA 31708

bearmanormedia.com

Typesetting and layout by John Teehan

ISBN—978-1-62933-341-0

*Dedicated to all the people whose
stories are yet untold*

# TABLE OF CONTENTS

# Author's Note

With the exception of the vignettes, in which I employ a touch of poetic license, characters' dialogue comes from contemporaneous magazine articles and newspaper reports. The Corliss Palmer affair was a minor soap opera at the time, and I had no shortage of quotes and interviews to choose from. "Herb" represents an anonymous source, and "Daisy" is an amalgam of the unnamed "friends" Corliss referenced in her serialized life story.

# ACKNOWLEDGEMENTS

First and foremost, my family and friends for their undying support and exuberance. So much love to you all, especially Mom, forever my biggest fan.

Christine and John Lindquist: your generosity and kindness cannot be repaid. I hope you are happy with the finished product, and you have my eternal gratitude.

Scott Routsong, Melissa Bush, and the Brooks County Regional Library: your super-sleuthing skills were nothing short of a miracle. You better believe that note is in the mail!

Mary Mallory, Cristy Sheehan, Jeannette Rook, Jamie Farrell Thompson, Ned Thanhouser, Jeff Joeckel, Scott Thompson, Paula Uruburu, David Stenn, Bob Craig, and Howard Kroplick: thank you all for playing an important part in telling Corliss' story.

Lastly, special thanks to the Media History Digital Library (http://media-historyproject.org) and Newspapers.com for providing tools essential to unearthing these stories of the past.

Two nurses stood chatting outside Edith Mason's door, sneaking glances of their new charge. She lay in bed, smoking, her eyes red welts below a mass of tangled, badly-dyed hair.

"Poor thing," whispered a smartly-bobbed blonde. "I heard they needed a straitjacket for her."

The brunette shook her head. "Nah, just handcuffs." She glanced at down at her chart. "Dr. Geiger says here she was real tight though, kicking and biting and screaming like she was crazy."

The bobbed blonde stole a look. "Edith Mason. You know I heard that's not even her real name? My friend saw her check into the Palace. Said she's Corliss Palmer."

"Who?"

"Corliss Palmer, the movie star. Remember her? She was always in the papers after she won that beauty contest…."

Thirteen years ago. Lucky thirteen. Corliss was a pretty Georgia girl then, with thick auburn hair and a cherub's face. Now her cheeks were wan, her forehead creased by worry and sorrow. "I want to die," she wept. "I have nothing to live for… too many promises made to me have been broken."

# REEL ONE:

## THE BEGINNING

*Every girl is born a princess, blessed by the fairies with*
*beauty, health, joy, charm...*
*at the same time, the evil fairy also was present with her*
*curse.*
—Corliss Palmer, "In League with the Fairies"

There are few things as boring as a cigar stand during the off time. *At least there was no shortage of reading material,* Corliss thought, thumbing aimlessly through yet another magazine. This one was *Motion Picture,* one of her favorites. She devoured the love stories adapted from the latest "flickers," which drove Mama crazy. "Your mind is gonna grow weeds!" Towards the back of the issue, something caught her eye: an ad proclaiming the "Fame and Fortune Contest for 1920."

"Fame and fortune. Could you imagine?" she murmured, envisioning herself swathed in furs and diamonds, laughing over lobster with Norma Talmadge or Richard Barthelmess. She already knew she was pretty. People said she'd gotten her job at the general store more for her face than for her skills, and she had no shortage of smiling businessmen buying way too many packets of Sen-Sen from her counter here in the Hotel Dempsey.

"Hey, Daisy," she called to a tall girl stacking boxes. "Have you seen this?"

Daisy wiped her hands on the front of her dress and ambled over. She pulled the magazine closer. "Yup! Me and some of the others are gonna send our photos in. Hey, do it with us! It'll be a scream!"

Corliss laughed. "Maybe I will. I have a photo at home I can send. It's not much, but it'll do." She dogeared the page and slipped the magazine under the counter. "Mary Pickford, move over!"

That night in bed, the envelope waiting on her dresser for the morning mail, Corliss dreamed with her eyes open. She mused on how her life could change… and how much it already had in the last few years. Before, the Palmers lived a simple but happy life by all appearances. Luther, Julia, and their six children rented a modest South Court Street house in Quitman, Georgia, right near the Florida line. Luther was a machinist in the electric plant, and Julia kept house—and kept Mary, Corliss, Hoke, Ennis, Grady, and Stanton from climbing the walls most days. Corliss in particular was a challenge, perpetually in motion like her namesake engines at the plant. It was a big, messy, noisy household, and they rejoiced the day Luther was promoted to supervisor.

One Sunday morning in June Luther felt odd. When a shot of his usual rye failed to perk him up, he decided on a bath. Police found him passed out on the bathroom floor; he'd never even filled the tub. "Despite the utmost efforts of his physicians," he never regained consciousness, and died at 3:30 am Monday, June 20, 1910. They never did find out what killed him at the young age of 38.

Julia was left grief-stricken and terrified. How was she going to support six children under the age of 14 with zero income? Thanks to Luther's estate they had a little money, but it wouldn't last long. Luther was a Mason, and in good standing, so she sent the kids to the Masonic Home until she found a new revenue stream, in the way most women did then: she remarried. The whole family (save Stanton, who remained at the Home) moved to the home of Julia's new husband in Macon. James Simmone's job as foreman of Allied Packers provided much-needed financial security, and he and Julia had three children together: Katherine, James Jr., and Julia Jr.

Corliss and her siblings were shaped by their mother's upbringing in the small Providence neighborhood of Jemison, Alabama. Chilton County, bordered by the Coosa River, was only ten years old when Julia Farrell was born in 1877. Rural and primarily agricultural, its plentiful pines fed a thriving lumber industry; the sawmill erected in 1872 employed much of the region, including Julia's father John.

Life in the Reconstructionist South was confusing and filled with upheaval. Affluent old-guard whites, secure at the top of the food chain, fought Black progress overtly through hate groups like the KKK and covertly through political disenfranchisement and segregation. Many saw

"Jim Crow" laws as necessary for peace. For the poor and working class, who needed as many family members earning an income as possible, education was dismissed as unnecessary and untrustworthy. In 1880 over half of Alabama was illiterate, and those who attended school did so only three or four months out of the year, up to sixth grade. Christine Lindquist, in remembering her grandmother, noted her lack of education—Julia never attended a single day of school—and her distrust of people of color. As the only constant in their lives, it's only natural that fervency against poverty and abhorrence of those seen "beneath" them seeped through to the children.

Corliss' thoughts returned to the present. There were fewer Palmers at Hazel Street now. Mary married Oscar Preston and moved out. Hoke came home from the war, took an Army job as a sentry on government property, and died via "accidental" pistol shot less than four months later. Stanton, being the youngest, was still at the Masonic Home. She, Grady and Ennis earned their keep, the former a doffer (bobbin-changer) at the cotton mill, the latter a stenographer at the Hotel Dempsey.

* * *

Eugene Brewster, publisher of *Motion Picture*, sat listlessly at the heavy wood table. He'd been rifling through photos for that infernal contest all morning, and whatever patience he'd had was worn through. Pushing his chair back to stretch produced a metallic *clang*: he'd knocked over the trash bin, full of rubbish—and one small, funny-looking photo. Brewster snatched it up.

"Lillian! Come here this instant!"

Lillian Montanye, staff writer and "mother reporter" at age 50, hurried in. "Gene, what is it?"

"I've found her. This girl... this girl is a living painting! She's like a breathing statue, an absolute masterpiece in the flesh!" He flipped the photo over. "Miss Corliss Palmer, Macon, Georgia. Why was this in the *trash*?!"

Lillian smirked. It was common knowledge that Brewster had a healthy eye for the ladies. Look at him, the man was practically salivating. She took the photo and placed it at the top of the pile.

* * *

Corliss was a finalist, the letter said, and she would need to get to New York right away for a screen test. Jubilation turned to consternation, and she sank onto the bed. She needed much more money than her paltry salary allowed, and she couldn't ask Mama, or James… wait a minute. She could ask Richard!

She'd met William Richard Middleton, a young and "awfully good-looking" government ship inspector, when he came to the general store to buy sugar. Truth was, though she liked him, Middleton was the one who dropped like an anchor. Deeply in love and wanting to fuel her dreams, Richard gave his grateful sweetheart just what she needed to reach the Big Apple.

The Fame and Fortune Contest was one of the country's first official beauty pageants, beating out Miss America by over a year. Promoted by *Motion Picture* and *Motion Picture Classic*, both popular fan magazines by Brewster Publications, it dangled infinite celebrity success in front of their largest demographic: young women. The grand prize promised to make an "internationally famous screen player" out of the entrant, complete with two years' worth of magazine covers, photo shoots, interviews, and "the sort of publicity that could not be purchased at any price."

Blanche McGarrity and Anetha Getwell were the first contest winners in 1919. Both starred in the Brewster-produced *Love's Redemption* (1920), a "society drama" along with poet Edwin Markham and inventor Hudson Maxim, playing themselves. (Maxim must've enjoyed being around beauty queens: he later served as King Neptune in the first two Miss America pageants.) It should not be confused with the 1921 film starring Norma Talmadge and Harrison Ford. Off screen, McGarrity was sold as a Pickford character, listed as 17 (actually 23) and photographed playing with dolls. Getwell was the exotic, with a supposed Russian heritage and childhood spent at the Czar's palace. After *Redemption*, McGarrity had a small part in an independent western and was "Miss Bluebonnet" in a San Antonio promotional film. Getwell did a little print modeling. Neither became an internationally famous anything. Anita Booth, a runner up, also went nowhere. Only Virginia Brown, aka Virginia Brown Faire, the other runner-up, lucked out with Tinker Bell in *Peter Pan* (1924).

Word spread, and by the 1920 edition more than fifty thousand eager thespians (including a handful of men) sent in photos. This time they were whittled down to a lucky group of "Class AA"ers and invited to *Motion Picture* headquarters in New York, where they were judged by Brewster and an alleged roster of greats: D.W. Griffith, Cecil B. DeMille, Jesse

Lasky, David Belasco, Thomas Ince, Mary Pickford, Hope Hampton, Lillian Gish, and more. About 700-1000 starry-eyed ladies from all corners of the country excitedly converged on the Brewster offices, where they were made up, photographed, and "instructed to walk into camera range, pick up a telephone, laugh, look worried, then terrified." Class AA was swiftly edited to 30. Corliss remembered being intimidated and "simply scared to death" by the chaos, not the least of which was: where were they all going to stay? Ever the philanthropist, Brewster insisted they all come home with him. There was simply no better place than Chalet des Lacs, the mansion he shared with his wife, Eleanor, and their son in Roslyn, on Long Island. There they'd be able to attend to work uninterrupted. Eleanor, daughter of Senator Cator of New Jersey, grew up around high-powered businessmen and knew how their minds worked. Eugene, self-titled the "grand smatterer," fixated on an idea or plan for about a year, drained the life from it, then moved on to something else. She figured the houseful of beauties was just another one of his infatuations, and she'd ride it out just like his law practice, his oil painting, the numerous books and pamphlets he was always scribbling, and all the other fancies. She also knew how easily a man's head was turned, since she herself turned his away from the first Mrs. Brewster. "My husband is a periodical love drunkard," she informed people. "For years I have served as Mr. Brewster's pitcher of ice water." Having Eugene at home meant he could work (and be monitored) uninterrupted. Besides, life at the Roslyn house was often isolated and dull, so she looked forward to her new friends—even if they were captive.

Working uninterrupted was a new angle for Brewster. If one looked up "dilettante" in the dictionary, the definition would be a giant photo of his face. Truly a jack-of-all-trades, and a master of self-aggrandizement.

Eugene Valentine Brewster entered the world on September 7, 1869, one of four children born to storekeeper Henry Brewster and his wife Clothilde. His gifts simmered quietly through a privileged childhood in Bay Shore, Long Island, then a haven of the upper-class. By his early 20s he was an accomplished writer and speaker, voted "boy orator" of Grover Cleveland's campaign in 1892. He worked tirelessly for the Democrats and in 1899 created the famous "Bryan Dollar Dinner" fundraisers for presidential hopeful William Jennings Bryan. Everyone he encountered admired his powerful presence and "remarkable magnetism of speech," especially at Princeton, where he spun enough plates to be on *The Ed Sullivan Show*. Glee Club, College Drama Association, baseball, lacrosse, varsity football... class, he admitted, was somewhat of an afterthought, and he only lasted there a year. He also attended seminary school for the year his dream was to be a minister. He threw himself into law and passed the bar in 1894, a year after marrying first wife Emilie Churbuck. Over the next seventeen years he juggled a booming law practice, lecturing, writing/editing books and numerous newspaper columns (including a legal one for the *Brooklyn Daily Eagle*), painting, drawing, opera and literature organizations, and raising three children. (I'm tired just writing it.) One other thing: Brewster created *The Caldron*, "a magazine of disdelusion," exposing the truth behind popular phenomena like anti-vaccination movements and astrology to phrenology, vegetarianism, and spiritualism. He somehow found time to "edit, direct, control, and publish" it starting in 1909.

Perhaps it was *The Caldron* that got Brewster talking with J. Stuart Blackton at a dinner party one night. Blackton, an illustrator and cartoonist, cofounded the Vitagraph Company in Brooklyn, and Brewster, fascinated with moving pictures, hung around the East 15th Street studio. The two debated the possibilities of this new commodity, and Blackton and his cohorts found the brash young attorney "compelling." They discussed motion picture publications—until that time, solely for those in the business, e.g. distributors—and decided to collaborate on a movie magazine for the public. In February 1911, Brewster and Blackton founded *Motion Picture Story*, with story adaptations of current moving pictures, photos, and a healthy sprinkling of ads. By 1914, as star bios and interviews crept in, they amended the name to *Motion Picture*. Reviews appeared in mid-1916, joining two of their most popular features: "The Answer Man," the first Q & A column directly answering fan letters, and monthly write-in contests ranking the popularity of actors and actresses. The frenetic and varied pace of the magazine matched Brewster perfectly, and afforded both men a chance to surround themselves with gorgeous women. Of course, they promoted their favorites: Anthony Slide, in *Inside the Hollywood Fan Magazine*, remarked on how many notices Blackton's wife Paula received from 1918-1920, despite having an "extremely minor" film career. Sales, and interest, were strong enough to launch the photo-packed *Motion Picture Supplement* in September 1915, renamed *Motion Picture Classic* that December. An atypical failure: *Movie Thrillers*, a 1925 resurrection of the film novelization format padded with original short Westerns and mystery stories. By June it switched to *Movie Monthly* ("the magazine with the punch!") and included standard fare like interviews and pictorials; a year later it folded.

October 1920 and, after all the preening, primping, fussing, and posing, the results were in: Corliss Palmer was the winner. She received the "highest rating given any girl so far," shocking absolutely no one who's been paying attention. What *was* surprising was Corliss' insistence that Brewster did not vote for her. "Mr. Brewster didn't care for my type, and had picked out a little blonde," she noted later, adding Mrs. Brewster had actually put her over the top. "She wanted me to go and live with her at Roslyn as her pal." The little blonde was 25-year-old Allene Ray, a "picturesque and typical movie beauty with curly, yellow hair." Indeed, photos of Ray—sometimes listed as co-winner, others as first runner-up—appear to have more star quality about them, and she went on to a moderately successful career. Four other young ladies made up the Gold Medalists, not winner's circle material but possessing enough "beauty, charm, grace and personality" to break out of Honorable Mention. Beth Logan, "a distinct type and a real discovery... slight of figure, with large, dark sparkling eyes"; Erminie Gagnon, "very pretty to look upon, with an unusual complexion"; Helen DeWitt, a "classic beauty, with golden hair and big blue eyes"; and Lucile Langhanke, "an amazingly well equipped girl, with sunset eyes and hair." If you know your classic movies, you sat up at the last name: Langhanke, already courted by Famous Players-Lasky, became Oscar winner Mary Astor.

The biggest winner to come out of the Fame and Fortune Contest was also the final one: Clara Bow. Years before becoming the "It Girl," the sixteen-year-old's soulful eyes and ragtag appearance charmed the 1921 judges. "Called in person—very pretty," wrote one on her cheap Coney Island photo. The other contestants laughed at her botched attempts at clothes and cosmetics, but Clara's authenticity and expressiveness stole victory. Besides, faces can be fixed: "Corliss Palmer made me up right."

The contest was over, and it was time for Brewster Publications to hold up their end of the deal. First step was molding the winner into a superstar, and for that, she must continue her close tutelage with Brewster. Corliss couldn't wait to get started. "I want [my acting] to touch the heart-strings emotionally... I want to make people conscious of their sympathies, their potential sorrows, and I want to do it beautifully and tenderly." Mrs. Brewster instructed the girl in fashion, beauty, and etiquette. She also became her acting coach, mining the dramatic skills she'd learned studying voice with Madame Valda. Performing ran in the family; Wilna Wilde, Eleanor's half-sister, was "The Powerful Katrinka" in the popular *Toonerville Trolley* film series. (You can also find her in the 1936 Three Stooges short *A Pain in the Pullman*.) Beautiful Eleanor Cator, the promising young coloratura soprano, read the *Daily Eagle*. Her parents bragged to everyone in earshot about that. That had been only two or three years ago, just before her sister, grateful for some writing work at *Motion Picture*, invited Brewster to spend the weekend at their estate in Far Rockaway (Long Island). Eugene and Eleanor were inseparable after that visit, and married in six months. Still, the thrill of performing "Lucia di Lammermoor" never left her....

In between her Eliza Doolittle sessions, Corliss was film cutter and general assistant to Brewster's own motion picture company. Brewster saw himself as another Griffith, and the beauty would be his muse. With his ingenuity and her lack of guile their future was limitless; his name would rival Edison, their productions Metro or Fox! Time-wasting multi-reel spectacles were "a passing fad. I'll be sticking to simple, modest productions; the story is the thing." Neither would there be any high-hat "society" pictures to gawk at; those just gave poor people "a very wrong impression" of the wealthy. Brewster Productions would be known for superior characterizations, acting, and art. And the stories! He already had a dozen in mind, drawn from the finest literature. Corliss and "Bruce," as she called him, spent a lot of time together, bent over papers, chattering excitedly. One could say they were inseparable.

\* \* \*

The ribbon on the Underwood was dry, so Corliss and Bruce rode into town for supplies. His leg brushed against hers as the car jostled along. She felt important next to him, superior, as if he were President of the United States and she his elegant First Lady. Bruce smiled at her, then ever so gently placed a hand over hers. Corliss jumped and snatched her hand away, eliciting a chuckle from Brewster.

"Corliss, can't you return just a little squeeze?"

"Why, Mr. Brewster, you're married and you have a child!"

They rode on in silence for a few moments.

"If I weren't married, couldn't you care for me a little?"

"Why, yes... I do like you very much."

She studied her shoes the rest of the trip, as certain secret hopes kindled in the driver.

Back at home, Eleanor sat Corliss down for a little talk.

"I've seen the way he looks at you, dear, and the way you look back. No, don't protest, your eyes tell me I'm right; but I think the best thing to do is to leave affairs as they are. You stay here, keep working and going out with Eugene. You forget, I know my husband and how infatuated he gets."

She took the girl's hand, still burning from Brewster's touch, and smiled.

"Don't be frightened. You might think me too old, but I understand. In a year we'll look back and laugh about this." She rose and crossed to the window, then turned. Her face hardened. "As long as no proprieties are violated."

Corliss nodded quickly and almost knocked over her chair fleeing the room. *Gene and his impressionability to a pretty face,* Eleanor thought. *Soon he'll snap out of it, and I'll do what I've always done: welcome him back like a mother does a disobedient child.*

\* \* \*

The situation simmered. Brewster, emboldened by Eleanor's seeming permission and constant distraction tending to their toddler son, Virgil, urged his protégé into late nights in the editing room. He stood over her shoulder, pressing against her, and soon Corliss stopped objecting. She no longer faltered at his gaze but returned it, lingering. Kisses—tentative at first—became brazen, barely hidden in the shadow of the stairwell.

One night, Corliss and Bruce returned from a jaunt around 11pm. This was not unusual, and they were used to slipping quietly through the dining room entrance instead of the front door. Brewster, one arm around Corliss' waist, turned the knob. It was locked. He jiggled it a few times, then knocked. No answer. "Eleanor must be asleep," he said. Harder pounding this time, then, in a timid voice: "Eleanor... Eleanor, wake up, someone's locked the door."

The sash scraped, and a head appeared at the bedroom window. A furious Eleanor, her face red and blotchy from crying, roared:

"IS THAT WOMAN STILL WITH YOU???"

Brewster kicked in the door and rushed upstairs. Corliss burst into tears and bolted back to the car. It's staggeringly hard to believe, but for the rest of her life, Corliss insisted she didn't see this coming, and that Mrs. Brewster's reaction was "the most awful shock that had ever come" to her. Was she innocent about a lot of things? Sure. Was she the victim in all this? Not for a moment. Self-exoneration was her trademark: "I had absolutely no idea what was going on," she said of that night.

Corliss sat in that car for over an hour, listening to the pleading, crying, shouting, and cajoling from upstairs. At one point Mrs. Brewster appeared, and Corliss froze; but Eleanor said nothing, only threw an armful of Corliss' dresses and underthings onto the dirty, oily garage floor. Shortly after the butler approached, his face clouded with anger. "You ought to be ashamed of yourself," he growled, "coming here and upsetting a happy home!" According to Corliss, he then slapped her across the face, hard. She cowered but did not reply. Later, after recounting the incident, she begged an enraged Brewster to forgive the man and not take action.

The butler's version... varied somewhat.

"You ought to be ashamed of yourself, coming here and upsetting a happy home!"

"What business is it of yours?" Corliss sneered. "You're only a servant, and a pretty bum one at that."

He slapped her across the face, sending her running to Bruce. Brewster, not exactly wanting the publicity of an assault charge, calmed the churlish girl and later comforted her with a new piece of diamond jewelry.

One thing both tales agree on: the butler was fired.

*    *    *

Eleanor apologized for causing a scene. She'd been hotheaded, unseemly. She and Eugene had patched things up, and everything would go back to the way it was, except for the obvious: Corliss could no longer share their home with them. Brewster set her up in a Brooklyn apartment, but after only a couple of nights, she returned home to Georgia. Panic gripped Brewster: he cared for Eleanor, he loved Virgil, but he worshiped Corliss, and her absence was agony. He sent telegrams to her daily, carefully disguising his name and location, but no reply.

Brewster paced his study for hours. For the first time in his life, he didn't want to do anything but remember sunshine glinting off russet curls, even white teeth showing in a shy smile. He thought of his wife and son, sat down at his desk, and drew a fresh sheet of paper.

*I have been through a most amazing experience during the past 15 months, and an almost unbelievable one. When another came into my life... I assure you that I fought it with all my strength. I thought of you being a faithful, loving wife; of my vow to love and cherish you as long as I lived; of our child and its reputation... but all in vain. We did separate [but] not one moment of happiness could I buy or procure. I could not eat or sleep and when she returned I felt that I could never let her leave me again, whatever cost. I have only the kindest feelings toward you, in spite of the terrible things you did to her, and I shall always do my utmost to make you comfortable....*

\* \* \*

Back at the family home in Macon, there was a knock on the door. Julia opened it to a bespectacled man, well-built, smiling sheepishly. He doffed his hat and offered his hand.

"Pleased to meet you, Mrs. Simmone, I hope I haven't disturbed you. I'm Eugene Brewster."

The familiar voice brought Corliss from the back of the house. "Bruce? What are you doing here?!"

"It's all right. I'm registered at the Dempsey under an alias. I've come to bring you home."

\* \* \*

Crimson stained the horizon by the time Brewster sat back in his chair.

"So that's my offer. Mrs. Simmone, if you and your daughter return back east with me, I'd happily set you up in your own home and give you an allowance for anything you need. Corliss, if you accept, you must promise me that you'll never vanish again. I need to see you. I need us to be friends."

While her mother prepared for her own exit, an elated Corliss accompanied Brewster to stay in a home he'd rented for her in Morristown, a fashionable suburb of New Jersey. Brewster wrote Eleanor eleven (!) more letters stating his position before leaving in April 1921. "My wife always thought me perfectly safe from the charms of others," he said. "In fact, I thought so too...."

# REEL TWO:

# THE MIDDLE

*"You have as much right to the pleasures resulting from the possession of beauty as anyone has."*

—Corliss Palmer, "The Democracy of Beauty"

The three-story Victorian was the grand dame of Normandy Park, the first built in the tony enclave. Even in 1887 it had all-modern accoutrements in its sixteen rooms, a wraparound veranda, and central curved bay projecting through the second and third floors. It was, like Brewster, simultaneously welcoming and imposing. The horrified neighbors were not as welcoming; accustomed to at least the appearance of gentility, they snubbed their noses at the latest inhabitants in the "First Love Nest." Brewster preferred Agapemone, "abode of love," and furnished it with only the best from Fifth Avenue and beyond. Breathtaking landscaping and floral trellises adorned the house's outside, while indoors "famous statuary was purchased abroad and sent across the Atlantic" and "noted artists painted expensive canvases for the walls."

Brewster commissioned five portraits of Corliss by Harry Roseland (1867-1950), an award-winning Brooklyn artist whose best-known work, *To the Highest Bidder* (1904), currently resides in Oprah Winfrey's private collection. Unimaginable decadence surrounded the former newsstand girl and her family—for Mrs. Simmone joyfully accepted Brewster's invitation, along with Ennis, Katherine, James Jr., and Julia Jr. "I was so glad that after all the hard times [my mother] had known she could at least have a lovely place to live in and plenty of money and nothing to worry about," Corliss said. Completing the household were several Borzoi, Russian wolfhounds. The slim, regal dogs were almost mandatory for the discerning Hollywood diva. Mae Murray owned one, as did Gloria Swanson and Pola Negri. Theda Bara owned several, and Nita Naldi joked she deserved one instead of her "full-blooded mongrel." (In contrast, an article about Clara Bow pointed out the absence of any Borzoi, cheekily noting her "scraggly" mutts wrestling on the lawn.) Corliss, a legend in her own mind, relished her new swanky status. "She used to strut up and down Normandy Parkway with her Russian wolfhounds," remembered Mrs. Albert Holland, whose estate, The Red House, was next door. "[Corliss] was a despicable woman."

One day, Corliss had roses on her mind. As beautiful as her home was, it didn't have enough of the fragrant blossoms to satisfy her. The groundskeeper recalled there were lovely ones at Cherrycroft, a nearby estate owned by banker Dudley Olcott and his family. He didn't think anyone would mind if she cut some, as the Olcotts only used the place as a summer home and it was often unoccupied. Corliss and Brewster thought it a fine idea and set off.

Agapemone paled in contrast to Cherrycroft's ten acres, nestled attractively amidst the other millionaire mansions. The caretaker welcomed the two and proudly showed off "sunken gardens, an Italian pergola, elaborate fountains, tennis courts, flower and vegetable gardens, hothouses and a cedar maze." Back in front, he filled their slightly weary arms with Corliss' beloved Maréchal Niel roses and invited them to return any time they liked.

To shut Corliss up at dinner that night took a stronger man than Brewster. He watched the words spill out, tinged with the twang she fought to eradicate.

"Oh Bruce, Cherrycroft is so wonderful!" She gestured wildly with her fork. "It's the most marvelous place I've ever seen!"

Bruce knew another marvelous place, snug between her thighs, and knew indulging her exuberance was his only ticket to an invitation. He laughed and patted her shoulder.

"We'll go back tomorrow, all right? You can stroll the gardens all you like."

\* \* \*

"The first floor is the drawing room, reception room, music room, and library." The caretaker waved a gnarled hand to his left. "The dining room's this way, finished completely in mahogany, and the kitchen and servants' dining room are to the rear. Practically every room has a fire-place," he called back to Brewster, who scribbled in a pocket notebook as they climbed the staircase. "Second and third floors are all bedrooms with private bath, even the servants' quarters."

Brewster snapped his notebook shut and shook the caretaker's hand vigorously. "Thank you my good man! Shall we go back outside and see what my little peach is up to?"

\* \* \*

"The next thing I knew, he had bought Cherrycroft for me," beamed the little peach. Brewster promptly put Agapemone on the market (it sold to the Weldon family, who renamed it Eleven Oaks in 1925) and held an auction in Manhattan for the contents. Most of the items showed their age; the tattered, dusty Victoriana went so cheaply that the auctioneer felt Brewster should've sold it in New Jersey and saved "cartage." Even the inclusion of some of Corliss' jewelry and an ermine scarf brought in little. No matter. Cherrycroft was still "furnished like a palace, with all sorts of art treasures, thousands of books, and so on..." She eagerly set about making it her home, aided by an army of servants Brewster hired for her. Brewster was a fixture at the new digs, doing everything shy of living there. A month before penning Eleanor's letters, he and Corliss, assisted by Lillian Montanye, established Corliss Palmer Productions, a $50,000 company focused on making the contest winner a household name. Long before the Kardashians, Brewster made Corliss a "brand."

Phase One: incessant publicity in *Motion Picture*. Mentions and "photo studies" of Corliss peppered each issue, along with her monthly column on all things beauty: care of the skin, hair, and nails, plus tips on diet, exercise, and overall poise. The columns themselves were fusty, florid, and almost certainly ghostwritten (possibly by Montanye herself). What twentysomething says things like "[j]ust as earth is impelled to put on a fresh mantle of green in the springtime... so is a woman filled with the desire to put into her person some of the youth and joy of the sea-son"? One column eruditely begins: "Last night I was beguiling the idle hours with Milton's 'Comus'...." Highly unlikely. (An aside: *Comus* is a story in honor of chastity; a subtle inside joke?) Brewster contributed sev-eral pieces for both *Motion Picture* and *Motion Picture Classic* with titles like "Impressions of Hollywood," always mentioning Corliss in the same breath as the current crème de la crème—whether about a practical joke played on her at a Marion Davies bash, breakfast with director Jack Mc-Dermott, or a dinner party for Irene Bordoni given by the Antonio Morenos. His bombastic editorials proclaimed the rest of Hollywood "just like any other city—only more beautiful" but noticed "many of these apparently beautiful girls do not bear close inspection."

Mildred Bowling, a fan in Baltimore MD, started the "Corliss Palmer Club." *Motion Picture* listed her address in their July 1921 issue and encouraged readers to "write her for particulars." Shockingly, this wasn't a publicity stunt: there really was a Mildred, and she indeed lived on Potomac Street in Baltimore. Hers appears to have been a hard life; she and her mother lived with relatives after her father's death in 1909, and both worked at a local casket company, Mom as a seamstress, Mildred as stenographer. By August 1922, only a year after her fifteen minutes of fame, she passed away at 21.

Corliss also gave advice on cosmetics. Purely as an aid to her faithful readers—"I am not in business and do not want to make a profit"—she offered her own personal blend of face powder. A finely-milled powder the color of a "ripe peach," it was not widely for sale but, if there were enough public demand, she might consider it. In reality, Corliss Palmer Peach Bloom was the first of many products Brewster feverishly concocted in the basement of his Brooklyn offices under the name Wilton Chemical Company.

Phase Two: saturate the market. Now that Corliss' name was synonymous with allure, it was time to roll out a new magazine, *Beauty*, to cement her reputation as an expert. Stylistically it echoed *Shadowland*, Brewster's labor of love aimed at the educated, urbane reader. *Shadowland* featured reproductions of and think pieces on fine art, literature, and music (both classical and avant-garde), along with interviews and portrait of authors, dancers, and prominent performers of the arts world. *Beauty*'s articles stressed the importance of developing charm both outwardly and inwardly; a pretty face meant nothing without, as Helen Keller said, that "light in the heart." Both *Shadowland* and *Beauty* shared the same unusually attentive craftsmanship: heavy gauge paper stock; quality inks; and clear, natural color. (I own a copy of *Beauty* Issue #1 and almost a hundred years later, it is nearly pristine.)

The similarity of the magazine to modern ones is remarkable. Mediums may have changed—smartphone apps instead of mail-order booklets—but the message remains: women must fight against excess weight, wrinkles, grey hair, aging. "Youth, beauty, art and romance enshrined" was the tagline, and *Beauty* was packed with tips, tricks, recipes, and, of course, lots and lots of ads to help you be just that. "Pretty... WHEN THE FRECKLES ARE GONE" shouted one for skin lightening cream. "Get Thin to Music!" boasted another for "reducing records," exercise instruction via the Victrola, precursor to Jack LaLanne's 1950s TV show or Jane Fonda's 1980s aerobic videos. Lucretia Borgia rubbed well-moisturized elbows with Helena Rubenstein; a stately rotogravure of DuBarry held court next to a portrait of actress/Ziegfeld girl Rubye de Remer; and, lest we forget, the full line Corliss Palmer Preparations, "art that conceals art," featuring:

- Corliss Palmer Peach Bloom Face Powder
- Corliss Palmer's at-home beauty parlor correspondence course, complete with "electrolysis outfit"
- Corliss Palmer Perfume, "her first choice of over 100 formulas"
- Corliss Palmer Face Creams, available in four formulas plus a "flesh" colored "foundation cream"
- Corliss Palmer Face Rouge and indelible Lip Rouge/Salve

All were accompanied by personally written directions, assuring "[y]ou cannot go wrong if her words are heeded." Though some of her advice is sound (powdered oatmeal in the bath to soothe sensitive skin), some was silly ("excessive laughter produce[s] unbecoming wrinkles... the smile is considered better form"), and some was downright dangerous (potassium permanganate, caustic if handled inexpertly, in a mouthwash recipe). One hopes no customers were hurt in their pulchritudinal pursuits.

*Beauty*'s masthead sparkled: Corliss, Pauline Frederick, Nazimova, Katherine MacDonald, and Jeannette Pinaud (possibly of the famous "Clubman" Pinaud family) made up the Editorial Advisory Board, while Lillian Montanye was Editor and Adele Whitley Fletcher, recruited from *Motion Picture*, was Managing Editor. Fletcher, who called Brewster a "frightful character," started as secretary to Vitagraph's publicity director and shortly after started ghosting. She was one of the most prolific fan magazine writers of the era, turning out almost three hundred articles and reviews for *Motion Picture* alone.

The elephant in the room: wasn't the whole point of the contest to make a new movie star? Well, all of Corliss' cutting and editing with Brewster was on three 1920 films she'd starred in: *From Farm to Fame*, a two-reel comedy about the Fame & Fortune contest; *Ramon the Sailmaker* aka *The Eternal Two,* starring stage actor Oliver Caldwell as "the great, hairy-chested, unkempt… brute-male sort of creature" that idle debutantes swooned over; and *In the Blood*, a drama featuring "society matron" character actress Leonora von Ottinger. The films changed distributors several times and, a year after shooting, still hadn't seen the inside of a theater, but Corliss didn't mind. While portraying identical twins on *The Thistle and the Rose* (1921), a prince-and-pauper story *Exhibitors Herald* thought "a sure box office attraction," a new appreciation of Brewster dawned. "I knew by that time that I was very much in love with him. He was so brilliant and big and wonderful in every way that I was simply swept off my feet."

Eleanor knew, too, and hell hath no fury like Wife #2 scorned. She filed suit against Brewster, proclaiming Corliss paraded around with "bare knees" and "vamped" her husband into leaving. Vamps weren't exactly something you saw in everyday life. They were Theda Bara or Louise Glaum, exotic creatures with heavily kohled eyes who crushed men like lilies beneath their feet, definitely not a former cigar girl from Macon. "Honest to goodness," Corliss asked Brewster after reporters packed their house, "I didn't vamp you away from her, did I?" "You did nothing of the sort," he replied, choosing his words carefully. "You have been a great help to me in my work; you are my inspiration."

Not everyone was on the same page. Corliss' sister Mary informed the press the two were already married, prompting a denial from Brewster: "[w]hy, that would be bigamy. I'm a lawyer as well as an editor, and no fool." Unexpected backup to Mary's claim came from Mr. Simmone, still furious over his wife's departure and refusal of his letters. "I have nothing to say in regard to my stepdaughter except I want it distinctly understood that Corliss positively said she was married to Brewster. She told me and her mother, and her sister also brought back the news from New York and spread it around town." Simmone was unstoppable and reporters lapped it up like cream. His wife sold everything in the house before she moved, he fumed, including the bed, without his consent. "She went away from me although I tried to persuade her to remain here… I'm not going to New York. I'm afraid I might harm someone." He ended by threatening to invoke the Mann Act: "[t]here are a number of [white slavery] charges I can place against Brewster, but I have no wish to do so unless they continue their attacks on me." Katherine's daughter, Christine Lindquist, explained why Julia so readily left for Morristown: James was having an affair. ("Attacks" on him, indeed.) Eventually he and the "Cajun woman," as she was referred to, ran away to Louisiana, and Julia disowned him, changing all of the Simmone children's names to Palmer.

Letters from Corliss to young Mr. Middleton arrived without fail, sometimes twice a day, dripping with excitement, love, and "lots of kisses." They sustained him during his sixteen-month stay at the federal penitentiary in Atlanta for forging government checks. "Please hurry and get out… I love you so much and think of you so, until it makes my heart ache and head ache."

"Maybe if I hadn't won the beauty contest I might have married him," she mused.

Middleton thought so, too, even with the strange chill in her last missive. Until one morning after his release when he opened the daily paper and saw his sweetheart on Bruce's arm, heard the talk of mutual adoration.

Confused and astonished, he rushed to New Jersey to plead with his bride-to-be. He arrived to locked doors and a throng of servants. He wasn't allowed in, they said. He'd have to speak to her by telephone.

\* \* \*

"I talked over our engagement with Bruce," she said. "You should forget me."

"Forget you? I couldn't forget you if I live to be as old as Methuselah!" His voice broke.

Corliss covered the mouthpiece. "He's just a boyfriend, like four or five I knew at Macon," she whispered to a frowning Brewster. "I may have given him hope we could be married someday, but when he went to prison that ended the matter for me."

Satisfied, Brewster took the phone.

"Richard? This is Eugene Brewster. I feel incredibly sorry for what has happened… I've seen all your letters to Corliss. But a great mutual love has come over us; I am going to marry her, no matter what happens."

It was a changed and bitter Middleton who returned to Macon. "It was like a bolt of lightning from the blue sky when I saw it in all the papers… I learned that she is absolutely incapable of any real love, except love for herself." Frustration tightened his jaw. "Still, he'd better marry her. If he don't—well, we have ways of handling folks like that down Georgia way."

Corliss fought no tears. "He thinks we were engaged, but Dick was a foolish, misguided boy. Plus he never gave me a ring like other boys did. I gave them all back; a girl has a right to change her mind." She did her best wide-eyed ingénue. "Mrs. Brewster No.2, I believe, got in touch with him. She got his name through prying into my private letters. That's the kind of woman she is."

Copious examples of the kind of woman Corliss was also existed. Eleanor recalled getting ready for an outing, donning her fanciest hat with "white ostrich plumes." Corliss peeked into the room and pouted at the attention-getter. "If you're going to look like that I won't go out with you." Exasperated, Eleanor proffered the hat. "Oh, I didn't mean that," replied Corliss, but she did take the hat, and (according to Eleanor) "wore it often after that." It was also Corliss' idea that Eleanor be relegated to the back of the car, an idea she vehemently opposed. An amused Brewster suggested they take turns, like squabbling siblings. "I was too humiliated for words," confessed Eleanor. Most of the staff at Chalet des Lacs disliked her; one housekeeper called her "very uneducated and ill-mannered."

One unpleasant incident speared family on the pointy end of her egocentrism. Katherine was fond of Mr. Brewster, thought him "wonderful, so kind." He was also generous, and when it was time for her and Jimmy to start school, he bought them both new clothes and shoes for the endeavor. When Corliss found out, rather than thank Brewster for his benevolence, she burned everything in a jealous fit. It stayed with Katherine her whole life, said Lindquist; "Corliss wasn't the angel [people] think she was."

The lovebirds sailed for Bermuda, a place Brewster frequently enjoyed visiting. For Eleanor, "a woman who Mr. Brewster says he has long since ceased to love," this was the final insult. Determined to have the last word, she sued Corliss in April of 1924 for "alienation of Brewster's affections," demanding $200,000 in damages. This, in addition to the divorce suit requesting $1500 per month in alimony. "On or about October 1920 [Miss Palmer] conceived and has since entertained a design of obtaining for herself... Brewster's financial support, affection and consort and of depriving the plaintiff and the said child thereof." At first, publicity seemed on the side of the star-crossed lovers, portraying Eleanor as cold, unmoving, vindictive. 21-year-old Marie Theresa called a press conference to defend her father; flanked by "best beau" Ken Lane and her Pomeranian, Chubby, she passed out a written statement to reporters, which said in part: "I can't and don't blame any one [sic] for falling in love with such a man as father, who has a combination of good looks and extraordinary abilities." "Let my wife sue," replied Brewster confidently. "She won't get a penny." Corliss agreed: "Worried? Not a bit. Let our lawyers and Mrs. Brewster do the worrying!"

Sympathy for the two quickly faded. Folks frowned when Mrs. Simmone headed back to Georgia without Ennis, leaving "only Brewster and the two young girls sheltered by the Morristown rooftree." They chafed at the couple's hubris, calling each other "echo of my soul" and "true mate". "He is my ideal," Corliss said of the still-married Brewster, "and I am his." Distasteful stories leaked: Brewster's request that Eleanor move into a separate part of the house with Virgil; his admission of being "infatuated" with Corliss, who "did not intend to play 'second fiddle'"; the girl boldly going about the house in his dressing gown and taking dessert with him alone in his bedroom. Sources at Brewster Publications, where Corliss had her own lavish office, said she put on "airs and graces" and meddled with editors, "most of whom feared to offend her." If Brewster put the kibosh on a suggestion—often to replace another actress' portrait with her own—tantrums ensued. The tension in an office where genial Eleanor once lunched with the staff twice a week was palpable. Inexplicably, Brewster thought it the ideal time for yet another beauty contest.

This time, having learned from their previous attempts, *Motion Picture* clearly specified it was *not* a moving picture contest. Run through most of 1923, the American Beauty Contest aimed to find the "Queen Rose of the Rosebud Garden of Girls." Entry rules were the same (send in a photo), as were the prizes: a "properly chaperoned" trip to Manhattan (or $1000 if the winner were from/near NYC), "well-known American artists" to paint her portrait and "model her head" for exhibition in a leading gallery, and her picture on the cover of *Beauty*. It, along with *Motion Picture, Motion Picture Classic,* and *Shadowland,* sponsored the contest.

The winner was Florine Findlay DeHart, a bright and popular sixteen-year-old from Bristol, Virginia, with "lovely blue eyes and golden-brown hair." The girl called "Flossie" by her friends had talent for music, writing, and drama but truly excelled in dance. Her classmates predicted a "phenomenal career" for their beloved class historian, thrilled that she chose to graduate with them instead of rushing off early. Her father, an attorney, gave permission for her to be "royally entertained [and] shown all the interesting sights of the metropolis" but only if she finished school first.

Three entries made Honorable Mention. Peggy Wood (1892-1978) acted on stage, film, and TV, best known for her Golden Globe- and Oscar-nominated turn as Mother Abbess in *The Sound of Music* (1968). Elva Pomfret (d. 1991) danced on Broadway in *Kid Boots* (1923-5) and *Sunny* (1925-6), then retired to marry NYU Dean of Dentistry Raymond Nagle. The Harvard School of Dental Medicine still bears their names. Kathryn McGuire (1903-1978) also danced but was better known as a WAMPAS Baby Star (1922) and for roles opposite Buster Keaton in *Sherlock Jr.* and *The Navigator* (both 1924).

While DeHart made the papers, their greatest attention was on an earlier winner. One syndicated piece couldn't wait to present Corliss as terrified, "sitting in her warm 'love nest' across the river... wonder[ing] if and how soon her movie magnate lover may transfer his affections." With no evidence whatsoever, aside from Brewster's Lothario reputation, they convinced the public she was about to be replaced. The same articles now delicately insinuated a sexual relationship between the two: Brewster "flitted from flower to flower," frequenting enough blossoms that he was now "an adept in the art of love," while the "once pure and unsophisticated" Corliss, embroiled in a love triangle, "had made her own bed—or had been assisted by Brewster in doing so." She went from prize-winner to Hester Prynne, "neither maid, wife, nor widow," and prudish fingers took great pleasure in pointing out "[f]or the 'other woman' in a triangle, sometimes the ultimate penalty is the public streets and the suicide's grave."

Perhaps misguided pity inspired Brewster's announcement that Corliss had cleaned out her offices and left for a "distant city" over a thousand miles away. The barest investigation revealed she was still at Cherrycroft, the two "constantly together in their motorcar," on a train to Manhattan, or in Atlantic City. Despite Mrs. Simmone's reappearance as official chaperone to her daughter, there was nowhere in the world where the "peach" wasn't a pariah.

Except at 29 Monroe Street, Brooklyn.

Emilie Churbuck had a name for herself even before she became Emilie C. Brewster in 1893. "A lady of brilliant intellectual and superior social qualities," she was as passionate about women's suffrage as she was "fancy dancing" (demonstrations of tango, waltz, etc.) which she often performed at fundraisers. The Brooklyn Democratic Club, the New York Women's Democratic Club, the People's Suffrage Club, and the 11th Assembly District Suffrage Club all counted her as a member. After marriage she founded (and was president of) the first Woman's Bryan League of America, wrote articles decrying sales tactics of department stores, and made it into the Brooklyn Blue Book, the region's social register. She and Brewster had three children together before divorcing in 1914: Ruth Bryan, Eugene Rafael, and Marie Theresa. Ruth, the oldest, married Duncan Dobie Jr. in a private beach ceremony in 1915; Dobie was now director of advertising at *Motion Picture*. Emilie, who still got along with Brewster, couldn't wait to blame her ex-husband's imbroglio on Eleanor.

* * *

"Miss Palmer is a sweet thing," she said, blue eyes twinkling. "The children find her a lovely young woman." She perched on a gilt chair, ankles crossed, spine erect, a textbook example of good breeding. "I prayed that another woman would bring happiness to him! We knew he couldn't be happy with *her*. Eugene does not like the clinging-vine type." She patted her perfectly-coiffed hair, as red as her brocade coat. "The Divine Power which takes care of everything will see that his present wife—I won't call her by name—will suffer for having kept Mr. Brewster from his three children and me."

Her home, the one she shared with Brewster for nineteen years, bulged with curiosities and *objets d'art*. She'd liberally covered the walls with portraits of her beloved Nazimova, the legendary actress. Her eccentricities encompassed everything from Esperanto to Christian Science to the study of "rhythmic rhythm... the art of being graceful." She was also an early adopter of *The Secret*-style positive thinking. "I believe if a person concentrates on things beautiful they can be brought about. I concentrated on Mr. Brewster's happiness... Corliss Palmer is an emissary heaven sent to answer my prayers. She understands his affection for his children."

Mr. Brewster was known to concur. Eleanor attempted to erase his past, forbidding any mention of Emilie or the three children. "Mrs. Brewster #2 made things pretty hard for me," he admitted. "I was never permitted to entertain any of my children [except Virgil]... I had to do favors for my former family secretly. Everything must be for Mrs. Brewster #2."

Emilie petted the tabby cat nestled in her lap. "Mr. Brewster could never stand that. And now, she is getting all that she deserves." She kissed the cat and placed her on the floor, then stood. "The children and I feel that it is up to us to help Mr. Brewster find happiness with Miss Palmer. That's divorce etiquette. Of course," she said at the door, "one can take it or leave it."

\* \* \*

Gossip effectively hobbled Corliss' burgeoning career, and Brewster resorted to privately exhibiting *From Farm to Fame* and *The Thistle and the Rose* himself at a screening facility on Seventh Avenue, a location still home to projection rooms and the Actor's Fund today. In the meantime, Allene Ray's career flourished, despite rarely being mentioned by *Motion Picture*. The skilled horsewoman and Pathe's Western serials were a perfect fit, and she performed all her own stunts. Rather reserved out of the saddle, the crew was forbidden to smoke or swear on set. They often had to deliberately scare her to make her scream for scenes! Ray and producer Larry Wheeler married in 1925, and both remained close friends with Corliss and Brewster.

The "magnetic darling" and her Bruce welcomed 1926 with a shocker: Corliss relocated to Hollywood—alone. Disillusioned by negative press, a stalled career, and still no divorce, she hoped to find better opportunities out west. A wounded Bruce refused to finance her, sounding more like an angry parent than a future spouse. "[S]he must be prepared to make her own way. She understands this and she knows it is for her own good." After stressing that only hard-earned success is worthwhile, he predicted she'd be home within two months. Corliss, undeterred, spent a sleepless night on the train, chugging towards destiny. "I was on my way to Hollywood, and I knew that I was going to be a star… I had all the confidence in the world."

First National signed her right away, putting her in *The Far Cry* (1926), a romance with Blanche Sweet, Jack Mulhall, Myrtle Stedman, and Hobart Bosworth. The thin plot, a love triangle set in Paris and Venice, was "much ado about nothing—or practically nothing" according to *Film Daily*. It did earn praise with its climax, a Romanesque gala filmed in two-strip Technicolor. This opulent party scene was where an uncredited Corliss probably appeared, though her "important role" was promoted in *Motion Picture* with a two-page spread. Right behind it came *Her Second Chance* (1926), with Anna Q. Nilsson as a wronged woman concocting revenge on the judge (Huntley Gordon) who imprisoned her. Of course, she and the judge fall in love; will she be able to call off her vengeful stunt at the racetrack in time? Critics found it tepid and "below expectations" but appreciated Charlie Murray's comic bits. A few reviews namechecked Corliss for her "unimportant bit" but, again, several syndicated articles highlighted her as "eagerly sought after." Despite his former posturing, one suspects they came from Brewster's pen. For Corliss herself, it wasn't much, but it actually showed in theaters, and she felt vindicated. "I got my chance, had my tests, and they were very successful." June Mathis, celebrated for discovering Valentino and at that time one of the most powerful women in the industry, felt "Miss Palmer [was] a keen, clear-minded, intelligent girl."

Then came the March 10, 1926 edition of *Variety*.

\* \* \*

"FREEZING OUT CORLISS PALMER: NO ONE WANTS HOME-WRECKER

Corliss Palmer, the Macon, Ga. beauty contest winner, seems to be having some difficulty in connecting with any of the reputable picture producing organizations."

Corliss stared dumbly at the page. She'd heard they wrote about her, but never expected this.

"Whether the sidestepping is just a coincidence cannot be learned, but none of the larger companies have given her an opportunity, despite the boasted prowess of the Brewster Publications."

"I was so wrapped up in my dreams," she admitted, "that it never occurred to me that perhaps all the talk about Brewster and me would stand in my way." *Variety* offered one last twist of the knife: "All of the daily papers the country over [are] referring to her as 'a motion picture star,' something she never was, and the chances are never will be...."

Once again, everything was falling apart. Who would put her name up on a marquee now that it was synonymous with harlot? Bruce told her not to worry, that he'd do damage control. In mid-April, he held a luncheon for the industry.

\* \* \*

"Thank you all for coming today. As you are aware, I have an important announcement. Starting today, Corliss Palmer will become Violet Buckingham." He paused dramatically. "Buckingham suggests strength, dignity, and aristocracy..."

A titter in the audience. A cacophony of throats clearing. Brewster glared.

"…and Violet denotes gentleness and sweetness. Henceforth, please refer to her only by this name in all future coverage. Thank you." He turned to leave the podium.

"Mr. Brewster, Mr. Brewster, wait! What does Corliss say about all this? Why is she changing her name? Does this have anything to do with the story in *Variety*?"

"Neither she nor I care to discuss the reason." He disappeared through the doorway amidst the crosstalk.

The crowd looked at each other. Did Brewster really think this would work? A little over a week later, they had their answer.

\* \* \*

MGM signed Corliss to a contract (though, notably, not as Violet Buckingham). They immediately loaned her to Hal Roach Studios for a new Charley Chase short. Chase's popularity as a comedian at this time rivaled Chaplin and Keaton's, so this was an unbelievable break for her. Brewster also returned to work, dealing with the sudden resignation of two of his best editors, Frederick J. and Agnes Smith. They'd been snapped up by his largest competitor, *Photoplay*, but the reason for their departure was still a mystery.

\* \* \*

"Christ! Where did you get this? *How* did you get this?"

The source smiled and said nothing, tapping a cigarette on the case's lid. The editor leaned across his giant oak desk to light it.

"Never mind, probably better if I don't know. This is going to make a lot of people unhappy, and I don't want to be one of them." They shook hands and the source left the office, blending seamlessly back into those outside.

The usual stack of newspapers sat on the hall table at Cherrycroft, *Variety* always on top. Brewster went to pick them up, tucking in his shirt with a free hand.

"Bruce, coffee's getting cold," called Corliss from the dining room. "You can read your papers later."

He stood immobile, his throat a desert. He opened his mouth as Corliss approached, but no sound emerged.

"What are you doing? I have to leave soon for the studio." She glanced at the headline:

BREWSTER "THREW" FAN MAGAZINES TO FILM CO.

"Bruce, you're scaring me. What does it mean? I don't understand."

\* \* \*

Fred's hand was still on the doorknob when Agnes pounced. "Thank God you're home. I need details! I've been wearing a groove in the floor since you left for dinner."

"Well, it's not good." He locked the door and flopped onto the sofa, still in his raincoat. "Pete Smith was there, Howard Dietz too."

"From MGM?"

Fred nodded. "Apparently Brewster worked out a deal with them. They give the Palmer girl work, we play nice with all their publicity."

"So that's why they cancelled lunch with us and only invited you to dinner! Ooh, I'd have given them a piece of my mind! Eugene just cannot think straight when it comes to that woman. Now he's going to foul things up for all of us."

Fred pulled a folded paper from his coat pocket. "He put it in writing, too."

Agnes slipped on her reading glasses and read aloud. "I, as President, Editor-in-Chief, and sole stockholder of Brewster Publications, have entered into a business arrangement with Metro-Goldwyn-Mayer... for a period of one year at least, MGM are to be our best friends... we are to favor them in every way possible... if we can not [sic] say anything favorable we won't say anything at all." She ran a hand through her hair and continued. "I do not believe in tying the hands of my editors and critics; but, nevertheless, here is a case where we must make an exception. Of course, you must do this in such a way that it will not reflect discredit upon our magazines, and it must not be obvious publicity... I know you will all co-operate in this matter."

Agnes tossed the letter onto the couch and looked pointedly at her husband. He knew that look all too well. "Believe me, sweetheart. I'll be drafting my own resignation letter tomorrow morning."

"*Our* own, you mean," she replied, folding her glasses.

\* \* \*

Nobody wanted to cooperate with Brewster's backroom deal, especially Will Hays. The man who later became synonymous with the morally rigorous Production Code was already attempting to clean up the industry, and he had a number of questions for MGM about this "arrangement." Studio mouthpieces weren't convinced a contract existed, much less for the $200 per week insiders quoted. It was an astronomical salary when other beauty contest winners-*cum*-starlets, like Gertrude Olmstead, started at $75 per week. In addition, to avoid Eleanor's recently revived attachment suit on Corliss, her paycheck was to be issued directly to Brewster. *Variety* asserted "Mr. Hays has made it plain time and time again that the screen has no place for notorious persons." The mercurial world of motion pictures rejected Brewster and Corliss immediately: Famous Players-Lasky pulled all advertising, as did Warner Bros., who additionally notified Corliss her services were "no longer required" for *Don Juan* (1926), featuring both John Barrymore and the first synchronized Vitaphone soundtrack. Irving Thalberg, playing spin doctor, cited her contract's loan-out clause and assured she'd most likely never actually work at MGM.

Brewster did not apologize or deny any of the charges. He stressed his victimhood, his letter misinterpreted and "fallen into the hands of [his] enemies," then poured gasoline on the fire by cold-calling press departments at "large film distributors" and asking their attitudes about the scandal. Annoyed publicists responded by asking Brewster's attitudes toward "any picture producer employing Miss Palmer other than MGM." First National became the third studio to pull advertising.

At the June convention of the Motion Picture Theater Owners of America, president Pete Woodhull suggested a resolution to "bar all pictures in which Corliss Palmer appears" and insisted on action against "unsavory notoriety instead of proper publicity." Secretary George P. Aaron announced the official "resolution of condemnation" two days later. News of this drew ire from the big guy, Louis B. Mayer, who blamed his ignorance up until that point on a trip back east. He personally interviewed Brewster and suggested "a nullification of the MGM $250 weekly contract [and] instruct[ed] Brewster to forget the letter he wrote to his editors."

Another dissenting voice belonged to Helen DeWitt. The Gold Medalist said she never received anything close to the publicity she'd been promised, and repeated letters to his offices went unanswered. *Variety* sided with the musician, calling her the "actual prizewinner" of the contest. (Guess they forgot about the other four ladies.)

Tamar Lane found himself crying in the wilderness. The writer, film critic for the *Boston Evening Record*, and editor of *Film Mercury* found all the pearl-clutching hypocritical. "One would think, to hear the shrieks arising from certain sanctimonious quarters, that such a tie-up is a rare event in the film industry." He suggested the list was inaccurate without naming more names, but dryly noted listing them was something the "'fearless' Crusaders will not be so anxious to assail."

Amidst calls for Will Hays to ease Corliss out "as the Hays silent system is alleged to have done for others," Corliss finished the Roach film, a Shakespearean spoof titled *Bromo and Juliet* (1926). She requested billing as "Corliss Buckingham" upon its release. She was also supposed to work on *Up in Mabel's Room* (1926) at Christie, but again was replaced. *Variety* ran a story on her replacement, Phyllis Haver, whose performance in the Marie Prevost comedy resulted in a five-year contract. (Interestingly, Haver also had a small part in *Don Juan*.) "I guess the studios were afraid of me," said Corliss.

Drama popped back up in her private life, too. Her sister Ennis vanished back in May, around the same time as local (and married) car salesman George Purtell. By the first week in July, it was official: Ennis and Purtell had eloped. Theodore Wilson, caretaker at Cherrycroft, told the press Corliss was "awfully mad [and] tried to break it off, but couldn't." Asked for comment, Purtell's now ex-wife, Margaret, stated "Ennis didn't get very much of a prize."

Now that Brewster was out of hiding, folks noted how fresh and well-rested he appeared. "At least fifteen years younger," read one opinion. Had the publisher accused of "knifing" motion picture companies gone under the knife himself? He wouldn't say, but people noticed another thing about the youth-obsessed businessman: "a rather long scar in the back of his head."

The rest of the summer passed quietly, aside from a minor kerfuffle at First National. Part of Brewster's letter about MGM referenced his wiring his editors to be "very friendly with First National and Colleen Moore, because they had done several favors for us." Was this why Corliss was celebrated as a "promising newcomer to the films," etc. for *Her Second Chance*? "Critics are knockers, plain and simple," said Brewster. "They think they are not earning their salaries unless they can find fault…."

Roach released *Bromo and Juliet* that September. Charley (Chase) is a reluctant Romeo to his girlfriend Madge (Corliss, billed as Palmer after all)'s Juliet in a charity show. It means a lot to her and Charley hopes his participation will get her to accept his marriage proposal. When Madge's dad (William Orlamond), also in the cast, fails to show, Charley finds him drunk—and keeping an annoyed taxi driver (Oliver Hardy) from collecting his fare. He tries selling a case of bootleg booze to raise the funds, but winds up having to drink it. He eventually rescues Dad, pays the fare, and they both return to the theater just in time to take the stage—completely blotto. What follows is a liquor-soaked travesty: Charley, the sponges he'd stuffed in his tights (to fill out his calves, get your mind out of the gutter) swollen thanks to a jaunt through a sprinkler, stumbles through sets, forgets his lines, and destroys everything. The audience thinks it all part of the act and it brings the house down! Madge happily takes his hands. "You were wonderful!—There were times when I imagined you had really been drinking—" Critics enjoyed the affable lampoon, and found Corliss a "most attractive heroine" in a role that demanded nothing else.

* * *

*Who let this schmoe in here?* Herb thought. He'd had the sandy-haired reporter underfoot all morning, didn't even go for a smoke.

"There's gotta be something you can tell me."

Herb sighed heavily and shut the file cabinet. "Look, I don't know where Brewster is, I don't know when he's coming back, and if you'll excuse me—"

"People are saying they saw him leave town with a girl." Mr. Sandy Hair leaned against the door frame. "He's been missing a week now, nobody knows where he went?"

"Fine. If I tell you what I know, you'll stop snooping?"

Sandy Hair grinned. "Won't even know I was here."

Herb swallowed hard. "Brewster went to Mexico to get a quickie divorce. He'd been planning it for a month now."

"And the girl?"

"Pretty sure he took Corliss with him, though you didn't hear it from me. Are we done here?"

Sandy Hair tucked his pencil behind his ear. "Yep, we're done. You have my word; we'll keep your name out of it."

* * *

October 20th Brewster emerged to corroborate the story, leaked to the press by an "employee". Yes, he and Corliss traveled to Mexico with a "woman chaperone" (likely Julia) to get the divorce, but this was no pleasure trip. Such difficulties they encountered! The hassles of establishing residence in Sinaloa, sleeping on the deck of an overcrowded boat, rough ranch hands escorting them back to Nogales, AZ... they deserved compassion, not disgust! Did he mention the ranch hands were armed?

In Mexico, on October 27th, Corliss Modena Palmer and Eugene Valentine Brewster were united in holy matrimony. They'd planned to wait until after Thanksgiving, but they only made it 24 hours after the divorce was legal. Larry Wheeler and Allene Ray were witnesses. Things were going to be much different now, according to Brewster. With Corliss his lawfully wedded wife, studios would relent and she'd be drowning in roles. He'd get out of the magazine racket and write scenarios full-time.

Dumping the magazines proved harder than expected. Brewster secretly finagled a deal to unload all five onto *Hollywood Life* publisher E. Wheeler Reid, but rescinded once it too leaked prematurely to the press. Brewster puffed his chest out with confidence, but his business affairs were a shambles. Besides the cancelled deal, Eleanor hit him with yet another attachment suit, this one for $50,000, meant to tie everything up in court while determining if his shady dealings in Mexico constituted bigamy charges.

Sixteen days ahead of the new year, the scandal ended. Well, some of it, anyway. The courts awarded Eleanor a $200,000 legal settlement, one of the largest on record at that time, and she cancelled all attachments and liens against her ex-husband and his new bride. *Beauty, Shadowland,* and *Movie Monthly* were history; Brewster was ordered to sign over the rights of *Motion Picture* and *Motion Picture* Classic to court-appointed representative Kimberly-Clark (yes, the Kleenex people) to "assure their continuance." Cherrycroft was also history, sold to Edward Schwab, brother of steel magnate Charles Schwab. Brewster moved Corliss, Julia, and "the family" into yet another palatial home, this time on 169 South Plymouth Blvd in Los Angeles, where Mrs. Brewster #3 "hoped at least we could be happy without having people making remarks about us." She threw herself into cooking, gardening, and entertaining with an enthusiasm that made Brewster sentimental. "Corliss has a very clean record. The worst she has ever done was to fall in love with me six years ago."

# Reel Three:

## The End

*Now as nice as this seems to the girl herself and to all be-
holders of her beauty, it is not going to be so nice in a very
short time....*

—Corliss Palmer, "The Slender Silhouette"

The woman who dominated *Motion Picture* merited no mention
in 1927. By April, Ruth's husband Duncan Dobie Jr. and partner
George Shuler bought back Brewster Publications' two remaining
magazines. (They changed hands again in 1937, going to Fawcett Publications; both Emilie and Eleanor continued to receive a lifelong weekly
stipend as per their contracts.) The sale marked Brewster's denouement,
along with Corliss, who never graced any of its pages again. "Mr. Brewster, who had been so rich and successful for so long, lost a lot of money,"
said Corliss. "[He] found it just as hard as I did to get a chance."

One chance she should have avoided was *Red Kisses*, an attempt on
the "legitimate" stage. The play, written by brothers Charles E. and Henry
Clay Blaney, concerns "criminals, crooks and rogues" evading justice by
working the diamond mines of Brazil. Later their community is enriched
by some ladies of questionable morals and a reverend bent on saving
them all. (Evidently the authors enjoyed *Rain*.) The original cast, including Charles Blaney's wife Cecil Spooner, toured select Eastern/lower Mid-
western cities; response was underwhelming but positive enough for a
west coast debut. A puff piece in the *Los Angeles Times* promised "some
of the most beautiful women ever brought together in one production"

at the Belmont Theater on April 10, with Corliss the main example. Notables: Sylvia Breamer, fresh from a short sabbatical due to an acrimonious divorce, or as the papers put it, "a breakdown following a strenuous motion-picture career"; C. Montague Shaw, already distinguished but still years away from all those serials; and stock theater veteran Henry Hall, later a familiar face in 30s and 40s Westerns. Also featured were prolific cinematic bit players Frederick Vogeding, Belle Mitchell, Frederick Vroom, and Tom Wilson.

"Flatter than stale beer," wrote *Variety*. It was bad (on Broadway, they insisted, it "would've lasted two nights") and Corliss was worse. "She has two lines in the first act and tries hard to put them over, but they just lay there." The unnamed critic intimated the whole production was financed by Brewster simply to give Corliss work, "who did not land in pictures." Even the chorines, always welcome eye candy, were terrible enough to "make any self-respecting dance director weep." The Belmont had a record opening night, even turning customers away... but they were there to gawk at Corliss, nothing more. By the second night there was half a house. *Red Kisses* closed April 22. An article the following day stated Corliss had received "two or three offers to return to motion picture work" and would've left anyway. (Uh huh.) It was later filmed (without Corliss) as *Picture Brides* (1934).

Looming debts forced Brewster to search for employment. Brewster being Brewster, he ignored the want-ads and instead placed one—"Who Wants This Man?"—followed by a list of credentials: actor, photographer, producer, author, painter, motion pictures, etc. "Experiences in all the arts and sciences tends to make an ever-useful All-Around Man," he stated, hoping someone would find him ever-useful. Several of the ads ran in various trade publications. No word if they worked.

Corliss, still technically with MGM, made *The Return of Boston Blackie* (1927) at Chadwick Pictures Corp. Boston Blackie (Raymond Glenn, aka Bob Custer) is out of prison and planning on "going straight" when he stumbles across a blonde (Corliss) who's just committed a jewel robbery. Insisting her "clear eyes" denote innocence, he discovers she is Sylvia Markham, daughter of the philandering John Markham, who gave the family jewels (ahem) to his mistress, Nellie (Rosemary Cooper), a moll for Blackie's nemesis Denver Dan (Coit Albertson). Sylvia's mother planned to sell the jewels to pay off her father's debts, and would be devastated if she opened the safe and they were missing. With the help of Annette (Violet Palmer, no relation), the private detective Sylvia hired to spy on Dad, they devise a plan to slip into the Markham home and replace the necklace. A complicated and at times rather slow series of events ends happily, with Denver Dan fingered for the theft and the jewels safely back in Mr. Markham's hands. Billed above everyone, however, is Strongheart the Dog, as Blackie's faithful companion. He dives from a carnival ride into the water, escapes the flames of a locked shed, and holds Denver Dan for the police; he's the best actor in the whole picture! *Return* also has the distinction of being the only extant Strongheart film to date. Reviews called it "not convincing enough to make it especially exciting," yet somehow found Corliss' stilted performance "sprightly." First Division Pictures, the distributor, would also handle two more of her movies, *A Man's Past* for Universal and *Polly of the Movies* for James Ormont Productions (both 1927).

*A Man's Past* (1927) starred Conrad Veidt as Dr. Paul LaRoche, imprisoned for euthanizing a suffering, terminally ill patient. After escaping he reunites with childhood friend Dr. Henry Fontaine (Ian Keith) and Fontaine's sister, Yvonne (Barbara Bedford), his boyhood love. Fontaine is going blind, and so LaRoche impersonates him, garnering attention from peers and love from Yvonne. When Lieutenant Destin (Arthur Edmund Carew) discovers and threatens to expose the ruse unless LaRoche gives him Yvonne (what about what Yvonne wants?), Fontaine shoots him—but LaRoche saves Destin's life, earning a full pardon. Corliss had a small, non-essential part as Sylvia Cabot. Critics liked the "tensely dramatic" story and praised Veidt as the "European Barrymore." It was one of his first four Hollywood performances, and the only one still lost.

*Polly of the Movies* (1927) was a female version of *Merton of the Movies* (1924), "an ugly duckling who would be a movie queen." The riff on "Fame and Fortune"-type contests starred Gertrude Short as Polly, an awkward maid who wants so badly to be an actress that she enters a contest—with beautiful Lisa Smith (Corliss)'s photo. The trick fails, but for some reason she's brought to Hollywood anyway. Angus (Jason Robards Sr.), the boy that loves her, follows and hires two fake producers to cast her in a drama. Thanks to her goofy overacting Polly makes a hell of a comedy, and when she is injured on set and lands in the hospital, a real producer rushes in and buys the picture. Polly and Angus make sacks of cash and live happily ever after. Others in the cast included Mary Foy, Rose Dione, Stuart Holmes, and Jack Richardson. "Inexpensive but entertaining," thought *Photoplay*.

Corliss' last movie for 1927 was *Honeymoon Hate* for Paramount/Famous Players-Lasky. The romantic comedy, more than slightly based on *Taming of the Shrew*, featured Florence Vidor as Gail Grant, the headstrong daughter of a steel magnate, who is "tamed" by new husband Prince Dantarini (Tullio Carminati). William Austin adds some humor as "silly-ass" would-be suitor Banning Green, and Corliss had a miniscule role as "Mrs. Fremont Gage I." Vidor's charm (*Moving Picture World* credited the "sheer force of her personality") and the opulent Venetian-inspired sets were the only positives in this rather weak and uninspired picture. *Film Daily* felt the talented Vidor "didn't get a very happy break."

Finances dwindled. "[A]lthough I turned back my film salaries to help [Brewster], they were a pitiful amount in comparison to what he had given me." Helen U. Hunter, a publicity agent Brewster hired to promote Corliss, resorted to small claims court for $50 back pay. Citing convenience, Corliss and Brewster moved from the Plymouth Blvd house into an apartment. The house, along with its "distinctive furnishings, oriental rugs, fine paintings and rare library" were auctioned off to the public, coming in (according to Brewster's numbers) $50,000 under value. First editions, prized oils and antiques didn't excite John Q. Public; one woman offered a dollar for a James Hart original worth $2000 because she liked the frame. The best performers were "two little bisque dolls appraised at $5 which brought $100."

1928 kicked off Corliss' most prolific period of screen work, beginning with a small role in *The Noose* (1928). Critics tripped over each other lauding the "heart-gripping," "tense [and] honest" underworld drama, "one of the year's best pictures."

Richard Barthelmess, a hot commodity thanks to *The Patent Leather Kid* (1927), is Nickie, a young man raised into crime by Buck, his bootlegger surrogate father (Montagu Love). After Buck shoots a rival gang leader, he reveals a secret: Nickie's mother is the governor's wife, and the boy better use that clout to protect him from prison. Nickie, in a blind rage, shoots and kills Buck. He is convicted of murder, but a public heartbroken over the sordid details of Nickie's life pushes for a pardon. No one is more sympathetic than Mrs. Bancroft (Alice Joyce), the governor's wife, deeply touched yet seemingly oblivious to any maternity. Alone in the world except for faithful chorus girl Dorothy (Lina Basquette), Nickie's end is imminent when a call from the governor's office stays the execution. Seems "the boy's mother was coming to see him."

*Variety* called the cabaret scene "one of the standouts." Filmed in natural light, it featured a bevy of beautiful dancers and actresses, including

Yola d'Avril, Kay English, and Corliss, who rated a close-up with Basquette. Thelma Todd, briefly attempting to usurp Nickie away from Dot, "only had to see that her very blonde hair was marcelled." (*The Noose* currently sits in the archives of the Museum of Modern Art in New York, unrestored and with Czech "flash" titles. Hopefully one day we can experience the "remarkably powerful" performances of Barthelmess and the entire cast.)

From here on, the quality of her projects declined considerably. She scored the lead in *Scarlet Youth* (1928), and the title alone should tell you something. It was a "sex drama," one of those titillating low-budget deals pretending to educate the public against the dangers of loose morals. The gist was the same in all of them: naïve young virgin is, through a convoluted series of circumstances, "ruined" and led into prostitution. Excessive drinking, drug use, and VD usually have cameos (bonus points for all three). In *Scarlet Youth*, an innocent country girl (Corliss) is seduced and lured to the city by a by a young man proposing marriage. After he reveals his true criminal nature, the girl, stranded and soiled, takes a job at Madame Celeste's brothel, where she is promptly infected with something appropriately nasty. These films, when not banned outright, were often shown in double or triple bills with other shocker-type fare like disaster reenactments or "miracle of life" footage ("it shows everything!"). Audiences were segregated, women during the week, men on weekends, no one under 16 admitted.

Movies like these were the life's work of S.S. Millard, one of the original "Forty Thieves" of exploitation exhibitors. He was a rumpled conman who served a year in San Quentin back in 1925 for "selling mortgaged property". Millard enjoyed flashing a fat bankroll in public but not actually using said cash to pay his business associates or employees, earning a permanent spot in small claims court. He came to Hollywood specifically to show "sex pictures," his first one being *Is Your Daughter Safe?* (1927), later renamed *The Octopus* by censors. By the time of *Scarlet Youth*, he was promoting himself as Corliss' "director and business manager." Neither he nor the film helped her already sullied reputation. "Pictures like this are the cheapest, shoddiest and lowest device for coaxing quarters from morbid morons," sniffed *Photoplay*. "It is no credit to Corliss Palmer and the other players that they would accept money for appearing in a mess of this nature." Her reply: "I feel that I have done a great deal of good, if by playing in the sex picture, I am able to keep some boy or girl from straying from the straight and narrow path." If only Ennis had seen it. (By now she and Purtell were the parents of an infant daughter.)

By March she was out at MGM and signed with Tiffany-Stahl. Her first film for them, *Clothes Make the Woman* (1928), centered around Russian Princess Anastasia (Eve Southern) ending up in Hollywood. It was a "weak imitation" of Paramount's *The Last Command* (1928), and critics thumbed their noses at it—but some exhibitors said it ran "better than ninety per cent [sic] of the program productions that the bigger fellows are making." Her role in *Clothes* was small, but more substantial in *George Washington Cohen* (1928), George Jessel's first feature film. The titular character (Jessel) is a "truth-teller which gets him into in all kinds of scrapes" (he cannot tell a lie, get it?). He finds and returns a wallet to Mr. Gorman, a high-powered executive (Robert Edeson) who thanks Cohen by hiring him as his secretary. When he discovers Mrs. Gorman (Corliss) is cheating on his boss, he tells him—and winds up on the stand during their divorce trial. In order to save a crumbling family, Cohen lies for the very first time, claiming he was mistaken. He is sent to jail for perjury but earns the love of the Gormans' lovely ward, Marian (Florence Allan). *Variety* remarked that Corliss was "still beautiful", as if she were ninety instead of twenty-nine. It turned out to be the nicest thing said about the picture. General consensus, summarized handily by *Film Daily*: "one of the stupidest comedies to date."

Then there are her two less than glorious "Nights." Raleigh's *Into the Night* (1928) had a tired plot—innocent father framed, daughter must save him from prison— straight out of the "mellers" of ten years before, and a tired star, Agnes Ayres (as the daughter), right off a messy divorce and in decline since the triumphant *Son of the Sheik* (1926). "Story wander[ed] aimlessly... difficult to follow," complained *Film Daily*. "Nothing to get excited about." Corliss not credited, not mentioned. Next, Reginald Denny and Betsy Lee fronted Universal's romantic comedy-drama *The Night Bird* (1928). Kid Davis (Denny) is a lion in the ring and a mouse around women, until he meets Madelena (Lee) by chance one evening in Central Park. Madelena is an Italian immigrant fleeing an arranged marriage, and her character is as backward and stereotyped as you'd expect: "But Meester, I no cana go home," reads one title. "Mario willa beata me some more."

Davis brings her home but his manager (a pre-*Dracula* Dwight Frye) sends her back from whence she came, turning his prizefighter into a lovesick mess. Next match finds him getting trounced, until Madelena's little brother shows up ringside, informs him the wedding is happening, and begs him for an 11th hour intervention. Davis KOs his opponent and races to Madelena's side, still in boxing trunks, to marry her himself.

Madelena's dilemma incited laughter, not sympathy, and Denny, who sparkled in light comedies like *Skinner's Dress Suit* (1926) with Laura La Plante, fell flat in dramatic scenes. You can find Corliss in the beginning as one of the attractive "dames" who unnerve Kid Davis at a party; he dances awkwardly with her for two minutes, then she retreats to her table. Not even a proper closeup. While some critics liked it ("Clever!" said the *Pittsburg Press*) and some didn't ("Poor!" said *Harrison's Reports*), the greatest reaction comes from an exhibitor in Texas: "screening the Congressional Record would give your patrons the same thrills." Another renaming attempt appeared on Corliss' contract for *The Night Bird*. She signed it as "Blondelle Malone," a name she certainly stole from the landscape painter Brewster featured in the October 1922 *Shadowland*. Whether the true Ms. Malone objected or the name just didn't suit, she never used it again.

One more downward spiral to the whorehouse for Millard, in *About Trial Marriage* (1928). This time the hook was "companionate marriage," aka living in sin, a hot topic of debate at the time. It spawned nationwide lectures, newspaper articles, and movies like Columbia's *Trial Marriage* (1929) with Sally Eilers and Norman Kerry. Yes, the similar titles were confusing; Millard took full advantage, subtly shrinking the word "About" in ads. Angry theater owners and distributors flooded trade mags with complaints and warnings to not be duped by inferior product. Finding reviews for this (or any other) Millard film is difficult, since they were condemned so often, but it's fair to say this didn't brighten the public's tarnished opinion of Corliss.

Out of all the work she did that year, her shortest—and arguably most charming—was a little piece for Fashion Features Studio. From 1928-1930, they released *Fashion News*, a biweekly five-minute newsreel showing actresses modeling the latest fashions, all in two-strip Technicolor. One of the surviving shorts featured spring hats and sportswear posed by Raquel Torres, Edna Murphy, Corliss, Laura La Plante, Ruth Elder, Jeannette Loff, and Barbara Bedford. Most of the ladies smiled comfortably, at ease twirling for the camera. Not so Corliss; her smile was pretty but static, her body language self-conscious. At the end of the segment she dropped the smile and looked offscreen, as if awaiting approval. That fleeting glimpse might've been the only one the world ever got of the genuine article.

The Crash. It wasn't kind to anyone, and Brewster was no exception. "The Depression wiped Eugene's wealth away," Corliss said. "We were perilously near being broke." Back in Morristown, Oscar lived with Stanton, Margaret, and Margaret's mother; Mary did not accompany him.

He worked as a gardener while Stanton did odd jobs, and managed better than most. Corliss and Brewster still owned most of Selma Avenue, their lovely place next door to Julia and the kids, and her final picture for Tiffany-Stahl was in theaters, In *Broadway Fever* (1929), offered in both silent and sound versions, Sally McAllister (Sally O'Neil) applies for domestic work after producer Eric Byron (Roland Drew) declines to audition her for his new show. She gets a job as a maid—and winds up working for Byron. Sensing an opportunity, she switches leading lady Lila Leroy (Corliss)'s train tickets from Oakland NJ to Oakland CA. When Leroy fails to show for rehearsals, McAllister dons a blonde wig and impersonates her until the ruse is foiled opening night. By then, Byron is not only delighted by McAllister but deeply in love with her, and lets her go on anyway. The routine programmer was variously described as "average," "boresome," and "uninteresting," and the players didn't fare much better. *Film Daily* enjoyed the silent version, but found the talkie "not up to standard." (Additionally, they called Corliss "attractive" in the silent but said she "failed to impress" in the talkie.)

A dearth of projects meant Corliss and Brewster spent a lot of time together which, as any retiree can tell you, can be a dubious thing. The bloom was already off the Maréchal Niels, as Corliss explained:

"Our romance began to fade not very long after we were married… it was just a lot of things all together. Our friends drifted away from us when we couldn't keep up the pace of entertaining and going places, and we were left very much alone. I had always respected and admired him but there had never been a real love between us."

Legal concerns over their Mexican marriage prompted a March 1931 one in Los Angeles, but by June she and Julia were in their own Hollywood apartment, and the only honeymoon was on the screen.

Paramount's *Honeymoon Lane* (1931) was an incredibly loose adaptation of the musical comedy hit. Eddie Dowling reprised his Broadway role, joined by June Collyer, Noah Beery, and Mary Carr. Tim Dugan (Dowling) is fired from his job as a casino dealer after his boss Baggott (Beery) accuses him of stacking cards so his friend Betty (Corliss) can win. Mary (June Collyer), his love and Baggott's niece, hears the news and leaves Dugan, who goes to a resort owned by loveable old Mother Murphy (Carr). Mother Murphy is struggling to pay the bills - or her employees - so Dugan offers his services as manager for free and pays off her debts with some of the $2000 Betty has sent him in gratitude. When a mobster and his henchmen visit the resort and want to set up a rival casino, Dugan suggests they advertise the property's hot springs as a curative spa instead. Dueling tourist spots, a king and his decoy, stolen money, Mother Murphy's cherry pies, and Dugan and Mary's engagement complete the plot. Keeping with current tastes, all songs were nixed save the title theme. Corliss' role as Betty Royce is small but pivotal; it's her actions in the casino that kick off the storyline. Critics didn't adore the picture, noting the vast discrepancies with the musical, but they didn't hate it either. *Photoplay* said it best: "Not a great picture, but a thoroughly delightful one." It was Corliss' last appearance onscreen.

The newspapers exploded that August when an exhausted Brewster declared bankruptcy. They'd tried everything to avoid it; Julia even filed claim to Hoke's $10,000 war insurance. Columnists piled on as many "Brewster's Millions" jokes as they could. At first, Corliss explained her absence as merely caring for her sick mother, but eventually confirmed the split, insisting it wasn't due to lack of lucre. "I know there are people who say "Oh, Corliss Palmer, she's just a golddigger [sic]'... that isn't the real explanation of the fact that Mr. Brewster and I decided to separate." Shortly after, the bank foreclosed on the Selma Avenue properties.

Hoping an image reboot could lead to new work, Corliss hired Albert Cohen, "handsome tennis player and publishers' agent," as her manager. Brewster shifted gears and offered editing services to new writers, 40 cents per 1000 words. "This foreclosure does not mean that I am headed to the poorhouse," he cheerfully remarked, and everyone admired how "smilingly and full of confidence" he was taking such hardship.

In April, everyone found out why.

\* \* \*

"It's true—Miss McCormick and I are engaged," Brewster proudly announced to the press corps. The lovely brunette at his side said nothing. "I met Dorothy and her mother back in October. She is an opera singer, actress, and writer. In fact, she believes so strongly in my literary work that she's going to help finance it."

"Brewster oughta give away dishes at these things," muttered one reporter to his neighbor, who snorted and coughed to cover it.

"What about Mrs. Brewster?" asked another.

"I will probably take some steps next week toward a legal separation from my wife. Corliss has told me she wants me to be happy and I suppose when she is ready she will file a divorce action."

"Miss McCormick, do you have anything to add?"

Dorothy glanced at Brewster, then took his hand. "Whatever Mr. Brewster says, goes."

\* \* \*

The silvery beaches of Catalina Island were the ideal place for an overworked story editor to escape with a special someone. Al Cohen thought so, and his wife Estelle might have too, if he'd brought her instead of a certain actress. To him, it was merely a good time; for the fragile Corliss, alcoholic and stuck in a lifeless marriage, it meant a brand-new future.

Estelle Albus Cohen, socialite daughter of Philadelphia manufacturer Morris Albus, named Corliss co-respondent in the divorce suit she filed that September. She also slapped Corliss with a $100,000 "alienation of affection" suit. Cohen denied the affair, which started around the same time Brewster met McCormick, and Corliss "had understood him to be unmarried when she first met him [and] when he told her that he was married… ceased seeing him except at his office on business." Not exactly.

\* \* \*

Corliss checked her watch again. *Almost two hours*, she thought. *What could be keeping him?* "Maybe I'll go over to his place and check," she said to no one in particular, stubbing out her cigarette.

"Hello doll!" Al opened the door a crack to greet her. "I know I was supposed to call, but…" He waved a hand to the commotion behind him. "I had no idea my friends stopping by would become a party."

"That's okay, Al." Corliss forced a smile. Al hated it when she was anxious or jealous. "But couldn't you send them home? I really wanted to go out tonight, just you and me."

"Tell you what. Why don't you go for a walk and I'll send these saps home. When you get back, it'll be just the two of us."

Corliss forced the smile again, nodded.

"Atta girl! Now get going while I tend to this crowd." The door shut.

She shivered and pulled her collar closer, tickling her cheeks. The coat wasn't fancy, but it was warm, and one of the few things from Bruce that hadn't gone to auction. Her heels clicked on the pavement, little staccato darts through her racing thoughts. *Who were those people? Why didn't he let me in? Was he ashamed of me?*

Her head pounded as she arrived back at Al's. She lit another cigarette and turned the passkey.

"Corliss! Uh... you're back early..." Al trailed off, his arms still
around a beautiful, dark-haired woman. Corliss, fueled by humilia-
tion and rage, pounced like something feral, tearing out handfuls of
the woman's dark hair, slapping the beautiful face. A strange wail-
ing filled the air and Corliss realized it was the woman screaming.
Al threw himself between them. "Oh God! Jeanne! Are you okay? Corliss,
what the hell is wrong with you?" He held Jeanne against him, both their
bodies heaving with her sobs. "Get out! Or stay here, I don't care. I'm taking Jeanne home."

Jeanne Sorel was born in Egypt and moved to New York when she
was ten. As a teenager, Sam Goldwyn saw her performing at the Capitol
Theater and immediately brought her to Hollywood. The exotic actress,
painter, and concert pianist was touted as MGM's new Garboesque jewel,
but instead here she was, a "Goldwyn Girl" with a few bit parts, standing
in someone's living room with mascara running into her eyes and clumps
of her hair on the carpet. Al threw her coat over his arm and led her,
stumbling, out of the apartment. Yet another door slam.

Corliss walked straight to Al's liquor cabinet and poured herself a
drink, then another. She sat in the silence, chain-smoking, wondering what
the next scene would be.

\* \* \*

A trip to San Francisco, Corliss told Katherine. It'd be good to get a
fresh start, maybe work as a hotel hostess or something. Katherine thought
it a marvelous idea, as did Al, when she went to apologize. He even gave her
some travel money and a letter that he asked she not read until she got there.
Now that she was checked in—as Edith Mason of Pasadena, to throw off any
news hounds—she sank down onto the bed and tore open the envelope.

*Corliss Dear:*

*Even all that has been said and done up until last evening, I still
felt that perhaps it might still work out some way or other. But I
am afraid that it never will, which you are also, I am sure. There
isn't much left to say or do. You can always count on me as more
than just a friend, and I shall help all I possibly can until you get*

*on your feet… [i]t is really a pity that such a marvelous friendship, such as you and I enjoyed for so long a time, must come to such an unhappy ending, but I suppose that is life….*

Corliss could not have chosen a finer place than the Palace Hotel in which to have her nervous breakdown. She lay in bed for days, drinking and smoking incessantly. The staff, fearing their deaths by fire or hers by alcohol poisoning, called a doctor and the police to escort her from the hotel. As already discussed… she did not go quietly.

\* \* \*

"You asked for me, Ms. Brewster?" Dr. Jacob Geiger, former San Francisco health officer and world-renowned epidemiologist, smiled warmly as he entered the room. He'd felt responsible for Corliss since the night the detention hospital transferred her here, to San Francisco General.

"Al," she moaned. "I want Al! Please get him to come; he hasn't written to me since I came here."

"You're not ready for visitors yet." He patted her hand. "But I will have someone wire him."

Weeks passed, and while more letters (and a dozen roses from an anonymous admirer) arrived, nothing from Al. By then Corliss recovered enough to sit up and talk with the nurses. "I chased the rainbow, and now look at me. Dr. Geiger offered to send me back to Macon, but it wouldn't be right. I can't go back to Hollywood, though. I'd hurt someone. I can't do that."

Brewster met Corliss at the train station upon her release, ready to usher her to the apartment her mother secured. They rode in silence, the trip eerily familiar, comforting.

"What will I do now?" she said softly. "Who can say? They tell me I was attractive once…."

They reached North Tamarind Drive. Brewster turned the engine off and looked at her.

"You will be fine. You come from the South, where people are reared to be thoroughbreds. Remember that. If you need me, I will come to you and do anything I can." He hugged her. It was fatherly; sincere. Corliss stepped out of the car but paused a moment at the window. "You were always kind, always true, always gentle…." She turned, before the tears fell, and quickly walked away.

\* \* \*

Al was neither kind nor gentle about Corliss, even after receiving the wire. He bluntly told the press: "As far as I'm concerned, it is no business of mine whether Corliss drinks herself to death in San Francisco. Any romance, that is, if there *was* any romance between us, is all off." His attorney Harry Sokolov hinted at possible reconciliation between the Cohens, but their marriage existed solely on paper, and his romance with Sorel continued.

Spring renewed both California and Corliss alike. Back from a trip to Portland, Oregon, she sat down with the *Los Angeles Times* for her first post-breakdown interview.

"I've finally snapped out of it. Often people get to the point where they think they can't live through their troubles. I was that way and tried to drown my sorrow in alcohol. But I am back to normal, thank goodness, though I feel like I am having to start my whole life over again." The profile of a placid, reserved Corliss vastly differed from the dazed, hysterical patient of only two months before. About Al, she said only that she might comment later.

Al and Estelle divorced in May. Estelle and their two-year-old daughter went to live with relatives in Philadelphia; Al and Jeanne married in June. (A second, rabbi-officiated ceremony, occurred a year later.) After the debacles with Brewster and Al, did Corliss even want another relationship? A 1943 issue of *True Confessions* gives us a peek. Not the best source, and most of the names are disguised, but other information backs up her story.

Shortly after her breakdown, she befriended "Dr. Roy Mason," an intern at Arroyo Sanitarium in Livermore. Concerned for her recovery, he recommended "a long rest, quiet, fresh air and good food," and invited her along on his vacation back to the family home in Portland, Oregon. According to the piece, Mason brought her to meet his mother, who thought they were engaged; Mason confessed he'd made it up to explain her company. Corliss didn't care: "[f]or two weeks Roy and his mother served my every wish. The rest and good food had a wonderful effect on my nerves." On their last night in Portland, the infatuated Mason asked her to marry him. "I've loved you ever since I first saw you on the screen." Corliss waffled, and Mason arranged for her to stay with his mother and mull it over while he returned to Livermore. Though he wrote daily, begging an answer, it was Mom who finally got through to her, via a hope chest:

"She began to lay out pieces of fine old linen, dishes and silverware. 'I've been saving these for Roy and his bride. Aren't they nice?'" The woman's tenderness towards her future daughter-in-law was too much. Corliss spilled everything, including the fact that she did not love her son. She packed and called a cab, scribbling a farewell note to Mason while his mother tearfully thanked her for her honesty. (During the earlier *Los Angeles Times* interview, she said her trip to Portland had been for "seeking employment.")

After falling back into alcohol and self-pity, screenwriter (and drinking buddy) "Betty Baxter" introduced her to "Roderick Demora," wealthy Arizona cattle rancher. He was married, but "his was the old story of the misunderstood husband." He was working on divorcing his wife, he told her, and so Corliss and he painted the town for a few weeks. When Betty had housing problems, Demora offered one of his in Tucson rent-free—but only if Corliss came along. "It was a bold proposition, the implications were plain," Corliss said. "Rod's name and money would again place me in a commanding position… 'Okay, we'll do it,' I said without shame."

Al thought he and Corliss were a flash in the pan. Problem was, he still had the pan. In August she sued him for a laundry list of things he allegedly kept after their split, valued about $2000 in total:

- four paintings
- brocade sofa pillow
- velvet scarf
- 2 books
- smoking stand
- candy dish
- Japanese cigarette box
- scissors
- cut glass wine decanter
- "extra-large" bath towel
- footstool
- wastepaper basket
- egg beater
- omelet pan

Did she really want those items back, or was it a way for her to waste his time, money, and generally be a pain in the ass? Al didn't wait to find out. Two hours after the suit went public he called and arranged to return her stuff the next morning.

Her next move was filing for divorce from Brewster, citing incompatibility and neglect, but asking no alimony in the wake of their "property agreement." Brewster, who wanted everything over quickly, did not contest, and the divorce was granted in December 1933. Corliss, whose life story was serialized for newspapers late that year, spoke generously of Brewster. "I am still very fond of 'Bruce' and we are good friends... [b]ut it just seems to be better for both of us if we are divorced." Brewster concurred: "She wanted gayety [sic] in the evening while I preferred to stay at home, studying and working. We remain the best of friends... I know that if I needed her she would help me."

While the Tucson house was being prepared, the former makeup mogul worked as a cosmetics demonstrator, insisting she was "genuinely delighted" to see old Hollywood friends. "I'm a changed girl," she again told reporters. "I'm working hard [and] through with all that foolishness. I think the future has something for me. Yes, I'm half in love now with a grand man, an Arizona cattle rancher." She smiled, her eyes tired. "At heart, I'm really a domestic sort of girl. I wasn't made for all this stuff I've been through."

\* \* \*

Back in Brooklyn, hard at work on a new project, Brewster discussed what else Corliss wasn't made for.

"She was exceedingly beautiful and exceedingly dumb. We tried to make an actress of her, but she couldn't act. She couldn't learn lines." He and the journalist sat surrounded by scientific equipment. Corliss Palmer Preparations was a distant memory, the lab currently devoted to a line of antiseptic dental products called "X-IT."

"Corliss was sweet and lovely, but that's all you could say for her. As for me? I'm all through showing off. I want to devote myself to serious things. I'm all through with love and women."

Brewster lifted a beaker of fluid, studied it in the light.

"Now this mouthwash of mine is a great invention, discovered by Mrs. Caroline Marsh of the St. George Hotel. You know, I've always had an affinity for money and I think I can smell it coming my way now... after I have made a little money with it, I will give the formula free to hospitals and dental clinics." His grin gleamed as brightly as his white dress flannels. "The simple life for me from now on, and remember, no women."

The simple life didn't exclude his passion for the pen. He spent night polishing his own manuscripts for sale, or hawking others' as an author's agent. He also returned to publishing with *Hollywood's Bad Boy*, John Gorman's novel about a divorced movie director entangled with several actresses. (Seems familiar.)

Corliss' pattern with men was also painfully familiar. Once again she was hurt when an unavailable man was, well, unavailable. Demora made clear she was nothing more than a diversion, and Corliss grew bored and sullen. After months of the "monotonous repetition" of party life—and months of evasion about his divorce—one of Demora's sons fell dangerously ill. He kept constant vigil at the boy's bedside, looking "worn and haggard" the few times Corliss saw him.

The man that returned after his son's recovery was irreparably changed. Fear and anguish made him "moody... grim and silent." It also drew him closer to his family, and when Corliss dared ask the divorce question again, he tersely shrugged her off. "I knew then that I had lost," she said. "But I wouldn't admit it to myself. I stayed on because I couldn't face cold reality."

Reality is often subjective. In Brewster's world, it meant fervently professing something—then doing the exact opposite. On March 23, 1935, in a private Jersey City NJ ceremony, 36-year-old Liane Hill became Mrs. Brewster #4. Only officiator Criminal Court Judge John Flaherty and two friends of the groom were present. Hill, originally from Louisiana, was a writer and literary assistant expert in everything from editing to typing. She owned a large house on Hancock Street in Brooklyn, which became the couple's home.

Corliss stayed in Tucson and lived with "friends," a whitewashed term for Betty and the revolving cast of ranch managers Demora sent for them to entertain. In October, after answering a want-ad, Steinfeld's department store hired her to model women's clothing for $5 a day.

Newspapers, burnt out from years of her expensive escapades, indulged in a little bitchiness. "[T]he girl who once coolly gambled a million to become a movie star and flopped," mocked one article, "is drawing better [as a model] than she ever did for the silent flickers." It was echoes of her *Red Kisses* debut as rubberneckers "watch[ed] her prance forth in everything from bathing suits to nighties" and evening gowns.

Her response was defiant, perhaps to convince herself: "I'm going to start life all over again. This time I'm going to make good. There [is] no use of my foolishly throwing the rest of my life away." The public's acrimony still stung. When Rosalind Shaffer of the *Chicago Tribune* interviewed singer Felix Knight and mentioned his hometown of Macon was also that of Corliss Palmer, he archly replied "it is the birthplace of [poet] Sidney Lanier."

She had an epiphany in her private life, too. "I began to see myself as I really was… [f]or the first time since I had left the Macon cigar counter I came face to face with Corliss Palmer. And," she said, "I hated her." Another note scribbled, another bag packed, and she went back to California. Her first stop was Julia's, a small, dark bungalow in Glendale she shared with Grady. "I dropped my head on her shoulder and cried for the first time in years."

*  *  *

"Feel these thigh muscles!"

"That's okay, Mr. Brewster, I'd—"

"No, c'mon! Feel them!"

Jerome Ross reluctantly leaned over and squeezed a thigh.

"I'm a better man today than I was ten years ago," the vibrant Brewster bragged, glancing at Liane. "In every department."

Liane shyly turned away, then secretly rolled her eyes. Attractive, "vivacious as they come [and] a sparkling conversationalist," she knew the game and happily indulged her husband.

Brewster's pamphlet, *100 Helps to Live 100 Years*, sold so well that the *New York Post* sent Ross for the scoop.

"A sensible diet, a sensible love life, and most of all, not losing your temper. Oh, and some chocolate about five times a day for that special feeling."

"Special feeling?" Ross looked puzzled.

"You know, vitality!" Brewster sat back and adjusted a white linen cuff. "My formula's all there in the pamphlet. I expect to live to be a hundred."

Liane murmured in his ear. He nodded. "Excuse me, I must get back to my writing. I write twenty hours a day sometimes. I intend to prove to the world that a man of sixty-five isn't licked!" He opened the front door for Ross, who had one last question:

"What about the bunch back in Hollywood?"

"Brewster indicated with a gesture," Ross wrote later, "what he would do to his fair-weather erstwhile pals…"

\* \* \*

The Brewsters envisioned themselves powerhouses about to set the worlds of literature and theater on their respective ears. In April 1936 they mailed a play to Arthur Hopkins (1878-1950), arguably one of Broadway's most successful producer/directors. While the plot of *Peddler's Lane* was insignificant, the *New York Times* couldn't believe what accompanied it: "a carefully prepared brochure" entitled *The Art of Judging a Play*, "in case Mr. Hopkins shouldn't be able to make up his mind. Mr. Brewster wrote it himself."

He also wrote *The Surprise Party Murder*, his first attempt at fiction after numerous non-fiction volumes on everything from Napoleon to Woodrow Wilson. The mediocre mystery, *Variety* felt, wasn't likely to "settle Brewster in a new and profitable niche." Unfazed, he wrote another guide to life, *How to Get What You Want*, and followed up by finding religion.

The Society for the Production of Ethical Plays sought scripts that taught "the truth of ethical and spiritual life as laid down by the Carpenter of Nazareth" without being stuffy or preachy. Their first play, chosen from over 200 submissions, was *The Well-Dressed Man* by John Dudley. Of course, Brewster also submitted a play, *Now and Then,* inspired by a painting of Christ he saved from the fire-ravaged ruins of the Roslyn house. Both he and Liane eagerly scheduled the Dudley play for the beginning of 1937 and cast Pola Borgia in the lead. Borgia, a nightclub singer whose best gimmick was her name (and the poison-locket earrings she wore to emphasize it) didn't appear to have anything but club engagements well through 1938; no other evidence exists to whether the play ever happened.

Corliss needed an operation—what kind, she never revealed—but doctors agreed she was in no shape for one. They prescribed a strict health and diet plan to build her up after years of drinking and neglect. "For the first time I obeyed orders," she said. Her constitution improved and the surgery was successful, but death still spread its wings over the Palmer clan. On July 24, 1936, Stanton, who had moved back to Georgia in the early 1930s, was hanging a sign at an Eschegonnee gas station when a coil of wire around his neck somehow contacted a live current, electrocuting him. Coworkers tried to revive him but he was killed instantly. It fell to Corliss to make the funeral arrangements which, combined with many solitary hours convalescing, led to an epiphany: "It's sickening and disgusting when you realize you are and always have been a selfish, vain person. Mansions, wealth, position, fame, all those things I thought I had wanted were suddenly unimportant."

She met "Claire Thomas," a cashier at a local café, and the two became fast friends. After a while, Thomas introduced her to William Taylor, a former rodeo performer. Rough and tousled, with legs bowed from "years in a saddle on the open range," Taylor was like no other man she'd ever met. The three spent time together, and, eventually, Thomas stepped aside, acknowledging something forming between Corliss and the shy, quiet cowboy. He showed up at her door on her birthday, clutching a long white box. Inside, nestled among the fern fronds, was a single long-stemmed rose. She knew what a luxury it was: after an accident ended his career he often struggled to make ends meet, and took whatever jobs were available. Corliss knew his situation but no longer cared about people's money or status: "it was their hearts that counted." They kissed, and she felt different; "for the first time I was thinking of what I could five him, how I could make *his* life happier… I knew then that at last I had found honest love."

*  *  *

The publishing was over. The Society was over. Even the dental products were over, after the American Dental Association cautioned consumers about its use. Mr. and Mrs. Brewster traded their Hancock Street house for a room at the Hotel St. George (Pineapple Street side). Brooklyn Heights had lost its shine by then, the Gilded-Age mansions carved up into boarding houses for the working class and "bohemians." The two lived frugally but happily, writing articles to stay solvent. On December 29, 1938, 69-year-old Brewster fell into a coma brought on by heart disease. Liane and Ruth refused to leave his side, even after he was moved to Long Island College Hospital. He never fully regained consciousness, and died of coronary thrombosis on New Year's Day, 1939. A small service was held at Fresh Pond Crematory, with only Liane and Ruth attending. A bad cold prevented younger brother Carleton, real estate mogul and former supervisor of Islip Town, from attending. Four days later, on January 4, he died in a car crash near his home in Florida.

Brewster "did almost everything under the sun and all unbelievably well," wrote the *Brooklyn Daily Eagle*, where so many of his letters and articles appeared over the years. His death "removed from the contemporary scene one of the most amusing, dashing, adventuresome, brilliant and delightful persons who ever helped to put Brooklyn on the map."

Corliss Brewster became Corliss Taylor sometime before 1940. "It hasn't been easy," she wrote, "[b]ut there has been so much of the one thing which really counts—love." The mature Corliss, her pattern of self-destruction vanquished, allowed herself to be happy—"happier than I deserve," she added.

Some would argue the wisdom of making such a statement.

The Taylors lived in a rental apartment on North Jackson Street in Glendale, a stone's throw from Julia's apartment on East Windsor Road. Grady, who had married and moved out in the late 1940s, died that March of a coronary occlusion. Corliss' own health was poor, worsened by a slide back into alcoholism, but something else was off. She was confused, belligerent. Imaginary things agitated her. In the spring of 1950, she entered Camarillo State Hospital.

Formally dedicated in 1936, the hospital offered rehabilitation services for drugs and alcohol as well as innovative programs for the mentally and developmentally disabled. Built in 1932 on the former Lewis ranch, it featured a working farm and dairy, bowling alley, two swimming pools, an auditorium, a driving range, and a gym on its beautifully manicured grounds. It was a popular detox facility and treated many famous patients, such as Oscar Levant and jazz legend Charlie Parker, during its 61-year history. With Mission Revival architecture and an imposing bell tower, some speculate it inspired The Eagles' "Hotel California." It closed in 1997, the buildings absorbed into California State University.

Corliss' official diagnosis was "alcoholic psychosis" (now substance-abuse psychosis) and "Korsakoff's (now Wernicke-Korsakoff Syndrome). Both triggered disorientation, hallucinations, and paranoia severe enough to be misdiagnosed as schizophrenia. In addition, the latter syndrome—a result of thiamine (B1) deficiency, a common side effect of alcoholism-related malnutrition—caused dementia. Camarillo's Department of Mental Hygiene provided "intensive intervention [and] specific therapy" to this population who, like Corliss, had limited independence and required full-time care.

Corliss fought for five months, until her weakened heart faltered under the strain. On August 27, 1952, at 6:40pm, Corliss Palmer Brewster Taylor succumbed to myocardial degeneration. She was 53 years old. Her remains were interred at Grady's grave in Santa Monica's Woodlawn Cemetery, and as of this printing, are still unmarked.

# PHOTO SECTION

# Opportunity Knocked— She Answered

MISS BLANCHE McGARITY

All the way from San Antonio, Texas, did this ambitious young girl come to take part in the grand finale of the 1919 Fame and Fortune Contest. She was unanimously acclaimed a winner by the judges, and her name and face became familiar overnight to every household in the country thru the medium of THE MOTION PICTURE MAGAZINE, THE MOTION PICTURE CLASSIC and SHADOWLAND. She is now as well known in filmland as any star who is backed by years of experience.

Do you think you possess the requisites for the screen? *Are you ready to answer the knock of Opportunity?* If so, cut out the coupon below, paste it on the back of your favorite photograph and mail it to us.

### RULES FOR 1920 CONTESTANTS

Contestants shall submit one or more portraits. On the back of each photo an entrance coupon must be pasted. The coupon must be from THE MOTION PICTURE MAGAZINE, CLASSIC or SHADOWLAND, or a similar coupon of your own making.

Postal-card pictures, tinted photographs and snapshots not accepted.

Photographs will not be returned to the owner.

Contestants should not write letters regarding the contest, as it will be impossible to answer them. All rules will be printed in all three magazines.

Photos should be mailed prepaid with *sufficient* postage to CONTEST MANAGER, 175 Duffield St., Brooklyn, N. Y. Send as many as you like.

The contest is open to every one, except those who have already played prominent screen or stage rôles.

Contest closes August 1, 1920.

------------------- MOTION PICTURE MAGAZINE ENTRANCE COUPON -------------------

Name..........................................................................................

Address.................................................................................. (street)

............................................. (city) ............................................. (state)

Previous stage or screen experience in detail, if any....................................................

.........................................................................................................

When born...................... Birthplace...................... Eyes (color)......................

Hair (color)...................... Complexion......................

Do you want to take part in the Five-Reel Feature Drama?..................................................

Entry form for the 1920 "Fame and Fortune" Contest. [MHDL]

Eugene V. Brewster, the "grand smatterer," in 1912. [MHDL]

J. Stuart Blackton in 1918. [MHDL]

The first issue of *Motion Picture Story*, later *Motion Picture*, 1911. [MHDL]

BLANCHE McGARITY

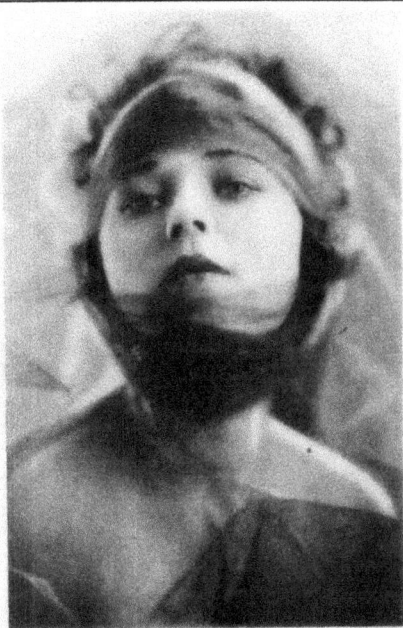

ANETHA GETWELL

VIRGINIA BROWN

ANITA BOOTH

Fame and Fortune winners, 1919 edition. [MHDL]

Corliss Palmer, grand prize winner. [MHDL]

The 1920 Fame and Fortune award. [MHDL]

Corliss (L) and co-winner Allene Ray. [MHDL]

A second Griffith and his pseudo-Pickford. [MHDL]

"Winsome Allene Ray" in 1925. [MHDL]

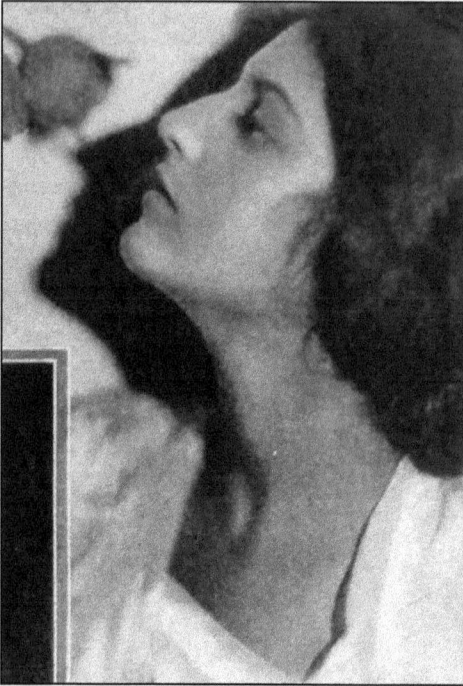

Gold Medalist Beth Logan. [MHDL]

Gold Medalist
Erminie Gagnon.
[MHDL]

Gold Medalist Helen DeWitt.
[MHDL]

Gold Medalist Lucile
Langhanke (later Mary Astor).
[MHDL]

Clara Bow at the time of her 1921 Fame and Fortune win. [MHDL]

Corliss and Leonora von Ottinger in In the Blood. [MHDL]

Corliss and Oliver Caldwell in Ramon the Sailmaker / The Eternal Two. [MHDL]

Brewster in his office, c. 1921. [MHDL]

Gibson Girl illustration by Brewster.
[author's collection]

# What's What in America

EUGENE V. BREWSTER

Editor-in-Chief of

MOTION PICTURE MAGAZINE, MOTION PICTURE CLASSIC AND
SHADOWLAND

Includes chapters on Christian Science, Osteopathy,
Dreams, Phrenology, Stage Tricks and Occultism, and
a section on Strikes, Profiteering and the High Cost
of Living. Cloth bound, 230 pages, mailed prepaid
to any address on receipt of $1.25.

## The Brewster Publications

175 Duffield Street                    Brooklyn, New York

Brewsterian bombast. [MHDL]

Emilie Brewster.
[newspapers.com]

Eleanor Brewster. [newspapers.com]

Eleanor and Virgil, c. 1920.
[newspapers.com]

POST CARD

*Dear friend:*

Please accept this as my acknowledgment of your esteemed favor. If you knew how many letters and requests for photos I receive, I know you would pardon me for not writing a personal letter. I am hoping, some day, to catch up. Meanwhile—my regards and thanks.

Gratefully yours,

*Corliss Palmer*

Address:
c/o Brewster Publications. Inc.
Brooklyn. New York

M iss *Fern Shipley*

*Belvoir*

*Ne*

A form response to a fan letter, with stamped signature. [author's collection]

Snow day: fun at Agapemone with Corliss, James Jr., and Julia Jr. [C. Lindquist]

Chalet des Lacs in Roslyn, NY. [newspapers.com]

Eleven Oaks, aka "Agapemone." [NJ Office of Historic Preservation]

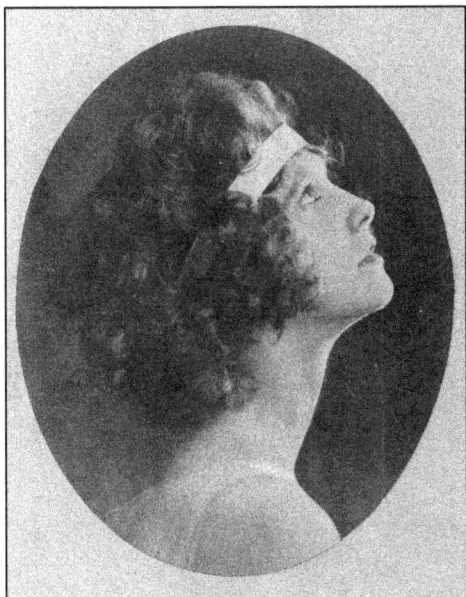

Florine Findlay DeHart, the "American
Beauty." [MHDL]

PEGGY WOOD

KATHRYN McGUIRE

ELVA POMFRET

American Beauty runners-up. [MHDL]

Ad for Corliss Palmer "Peach Bloom" Powder, c. 1921. [MHDL]

Cherrycroft captured in family photos. [C. Lindquist]

Cherrycroft. [NJ Office of Historic Preservation]

The Cherrycroft carriage house before remodeling, c. 1995. [NJ Office of
Historic Preservation]

The infamous Cherrycroft garage, c. 1995. [NJ Office of Historic Preservation]

Corliss and one of her Borzoi. [MHDL]

"I am very happy and completely satisfied, because I have got everything I started out to get. If my husband's little four-leaf clover still wants him where she is neither wife nor maid, she can have him."
—*Mrs. Brewster, the Injured Wife.*

"My cup of joy is running over and I am deliciously happy, for he's mine, all mine, at last."
—*Corliss Palmer, the "Other Woman."*

"The settlement of the case is wholly satisfactory to me, and I feel that I have been the chief gainer from it all."
—*Eugene V. Brewster.*

Gossip girl: an illustration of the Corliss/Eleanor/Brewster triangle. [newspapers.com]

Frederick James and Agnes Smith, c. 1925. [MHDL]

Lillian Montanye in 1918. [MHDL]

Detail from one of five Harry Roseland portraits. [public domain]

"Bruce" and his "peach" in 1931. [newspapers.com]

"Camera studies" from *Motion Picture*, 1921-22. [MHDL]

Ad for *About Trial Marriage*. Note the tiny "About." [MHDL]

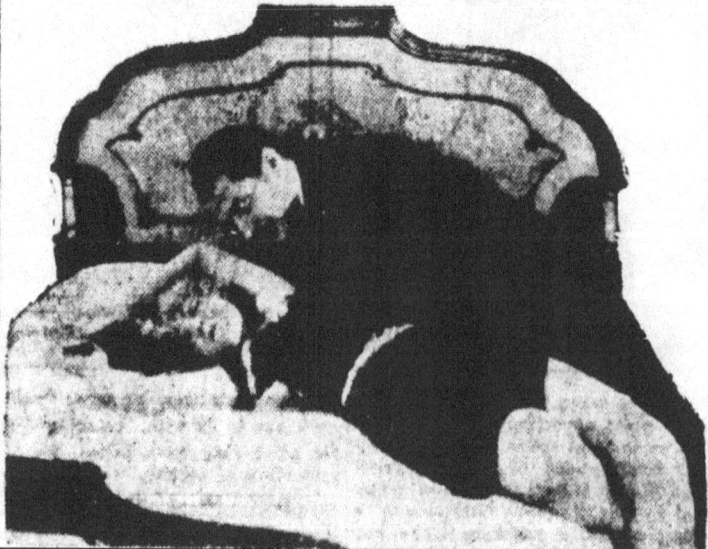

Peril awaits Corliss in *Scarlet Youth*. [newspapers.com]

Corliss and Brewster at auction. [newspapers.com]

Mansion's gone but the dishes ain't: the Brewsters in 1931. [newspapers.com]

Dorothy McCormick.
[newspapers.com]

Liane Hill and Brewster.
[newspapers.com]

Al Cohen in 1940. [MHDL]

Jeanne Sorel. [newspapers.com]

Estelle Cohen. [newspapers.com]

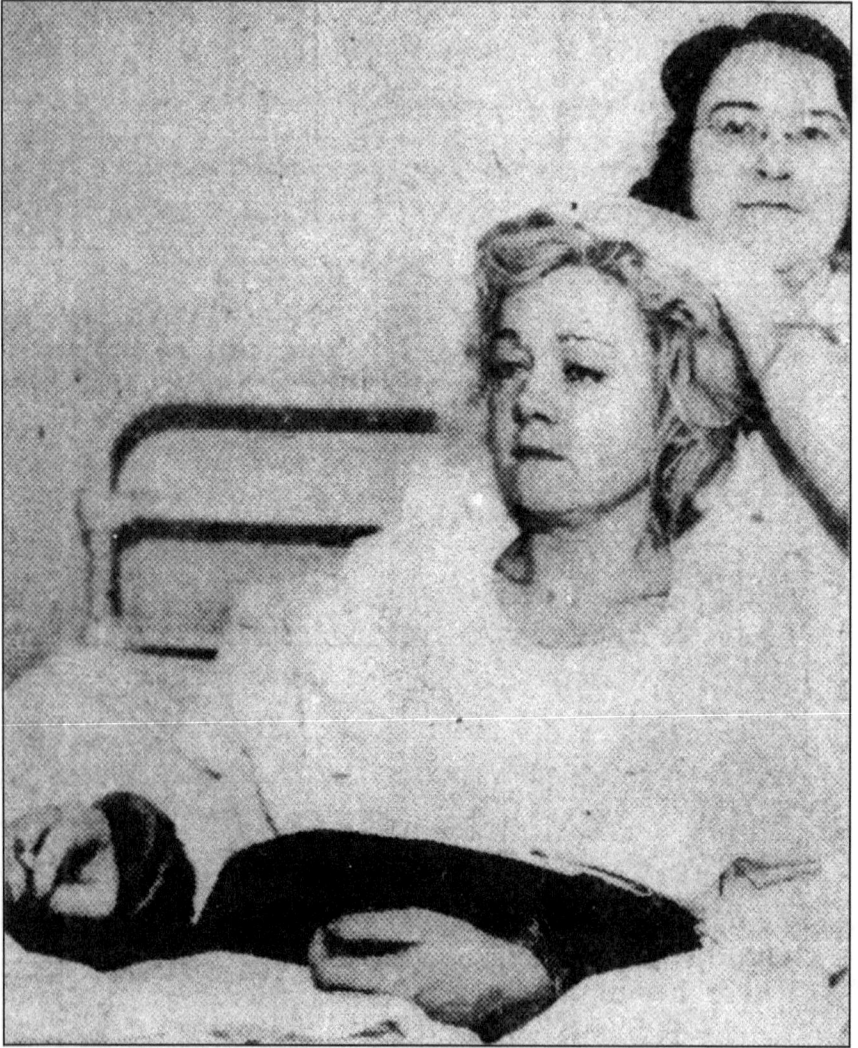

Peach, crumbled: in leather handcuffs with nurse Helen Nelson. [newspapers.com]

Hoke Palmer, c. 1917. [C. Lindquist]

Grady Palmer, c. 1923.
[C. Lindquist]

Ennis Palmer in 1926. [newspapers.com]

Ruth (L), Marie Theresa, and Brewster in 1931. [newspapers.com]

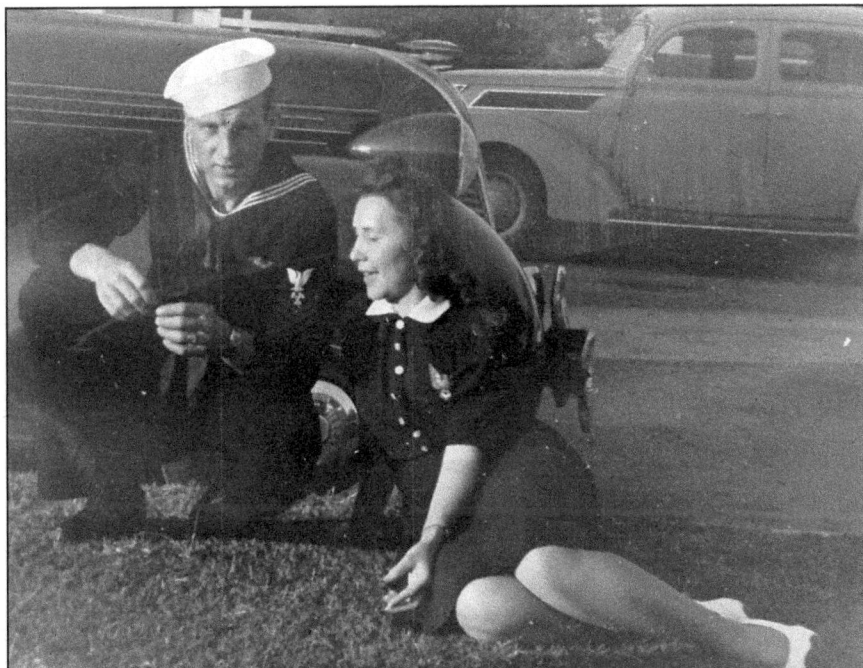

A grown Katherine and husband Al Frederickson. [C. Lindquist]

James Jr.(L), Julia Jr. (standing), and Katherine Simmone Palmer, c. 1924. [C. Lindquist]

Peggy Hopkins Joyce.
[MHDL]

Peaches Browning. [public domain]

Carol Dempster. [MHDL]

Fay Lanphier.
[newspapers.com]

Hazel Keener. [MHDL]

Mary Nolan. [MHDL]

# Scuttlebutt Sidekicks:

# A One-Reel Short

*What becomes of a 'queen' after her few hours of sham importance is over, is no concern of her exploiters.*

—"A Typical Finish," *Detroit Free Press*, February 2, 1933

An obvious parallel to the Corliss and Brewster saga is *Citizen Kane* (1941). Most people think Orson Welles' masterpiece is a thinly-veiled biography of William Randolph Hearst and his mistress, actress Marion Davies. Hearst thought so, too, and banned mention of it in his newspapers. But Davies was no Susan Alexander; she had talent, and was particularly skilled at comedy. One viewing of *The Patsy* or *Show People* (both 1928) will convince you.

There are also shades of the Evelyn Nesbit case, another instance of wealthy men treating an underage girl as a toy, devoid of purpose other than their satiety and amusement. (At least Corliss' situation didn't end in gunshots.) Here are some other stories sharing space with her in the Jazz Age gossip columns:

### PEGGY HOPKINS JOYCE

While Corliss insisted she wasn't a gold-digger, the epithet was music to Joyce's ears. Born Marguerite Upton in Norfolk, VA, she ran away at 16 to join a vaudeville troupe and perfect her engagingly naughty image. The beauty married her first husband that same year and left him shortly after; Hubby #2 followed quickly but was over by 1915. Joyce could not be contained: her outrageous behavior and lavish costumes kept her headlining despite any discernible acting, singing, or dancing talent. By 1917, after playing the Palace (!) with her one-woman fashion parade *Style Show*, she was a glamorous Ziegfeld girl. One year later she married Hubby #3 and ran through the millionaire's coffers so rapidly that by 1920 he was bankrupt. By her death in 1957 she'd collected six husbands, seven films, affairs with Chaplin, Chrysler, and Irving Thalberg, cars, jewels, furs... even song lyrics by Cole Porter, Rodgers & Hart, and Irving Berlin. Though debt and alcoholism marred her later years, her legacy as one of the first celebrities "famous for being famous" remains. "Better to be mercenary," as she said, "than miserable."

## PEACHES BROWNING

What is it with prosperous businessmen and lovely young things? Edward "Daddy" Browning had an incurable weakness for them. First there was Adele Bowen, showered in her heart's desires. When she wanted a child, he ran an ad in the paper for one. They adopted Marjorie & Dorothy, nicknamed "Sunshine". Sunshine stayed with Daddy after Bowen left him for her dentist. Since Marjorie went with Mom, Daddy placed another ad— this time adopting a companion for his lonely daughter. When 16-year-old Mary Spas turned out to be a 21-year-old aspiring actress, he annulled the adoption and focused on charity work instead, with—shocking—the local high school sorority. Here he met Frances Heenan, a chubby strawberry blonde with "piano legs" and a peaches-and-cream complexion.

Thirty-seven days later, on April 10 1926, 15-yr-old "Peaches" and 51-yr-old Daddy married. The tabloids went wild and so did Peaches, scooping up $30K worth of clothes and jewelry before leaving him in October. Their on-again, off-again relationship peaked with a months-long divorce trial bursting with lascivious details: acid attacks, pornography, pet geese in the bedroom, an "occult" woman wearing a pet snake, copious alcohol consumption. "My innocent sensibilities were astonished," wept Peaches. Browning, for his part, claimed the marriage was in name only and that he'd spent the entire time playing manservant to his gold-digger wife and her mother, who lived with them. The courts sided with Browning, and Peaches parlayed her infamy into a vaudeville career. She married three times more, all ending in divorce, and became an alcoholic. She died in 1956 after a fall in her bathroom resulted in a head injury; she was just 46.

## CAROL DEMPSTER

D.W. Griffith discovered Dempster during a performance of the famed Denishawn Dance Company, and cast her as the Favorite of the Harem in the Babylonian sequence of *Intolerance* (1916). As the teens faded, the smitten Griffith edged out the Gish sisters and Mae Marsh, choosing Dempster as his leading lady in films like *The Love Flower* (1920) and *Isn't Life Wonderful?* (1924). Problem was, her colleagues couldn't stand her, and neither could critics: "as an actress," Burns Mantle wrote famously in *Photoplay*, "Miss Dempster is an excellent high diver." (Ouch.) It was all Dempster's style: she didn't have any, save sub-par imitation of Lillian Gish and Mae Marsh. The "Answer Man" in *Motion Picture* thought her "just fair" and "lack[ing] winsomeness and grace." In total she made 16 films, all for Griffith except for *The Hope Chest* (1918), which featured most of the Griffith company, and the John Barrymore *Sherlock Holmes* (1922). She retired after *The Sorrows of Satan* (1926) with Ricardo Cortez, married a wealthy banker, and lived in blissful obscurity. In 1991, a few years before her death, she visited the Museum of Modern Art in New York to donate photos. As Anthony Slide mentioned in *Silent Players,* she suddenly felt the weight of the years and sent her husband to meet the staff instead.

## FAY LANPHIER

Fay Lanphier was born in Los Angeles in 1905, and in 1924 won the Miss California title at the inaugural pageant in Santa Cruz. That same year she came in third at the Miss America Pageant; by 1925 she was crowned both Miss America and Miss Rose Queen, the only person to do so to date. Lanphier signed with Paramount after an initial local film company contract expired, but only made two films: Famous Players-Lasky's *The American Venus* (1926), a takeoff of the Miss America contest starring Esther Ralston, Ford Sterling, Ernest Torrence, and Louise Brooks, and *Flying Elephants* (1928), a Laurel & Hardy short for Hal Roach.

Bad publicity followed her like a shadow. Her manager arranged a press junket complete with appearance fees, angering the Miss America organization who governed these things (including said fees). Some whispered she was a plant from the movie studios, and former Miss America Ruth Malcomson refused to work with a "professional." The notorious *New York Graphic* ran articles claiming both the Miss California and Miss America pageants were "fixed" in Lanphier's favor. She and the pageant sued for libel—and won—but it tainted her enough for Paramount to drop her. She toured successfully as a dancer for a while, and then acted with the Henry Duffy Players in San Francisco. Her messy first marriage, to Spiegel scion Sidney Spiegel, lasted less than a year; her second was a happy one and resulted in two daughters. Still, amid the good news, there remained a touch of schadenfreude in later articles about Lanphier. In the 1930s, they loved running photos of her, pointing out her twenty pound weight gain and stenography job at Paramount, the studio that was supposed to make her a star. She brushed it off: 'I like the work. I was a stenographer before... [i]t keeps me occupied and I am making friends.' She eventually retired and led a quiet life raising her family. Fay Lanphier died of viral pneumonia in 1959.

## Hazel Keener

"Hazel Keener has won so many beauty prizes," wrote *Picture Play* back in 1925, "that it isn't news any more [sic] when she grabs off another." The brunette Iowan was only fourteen when she won an honor roll position in the 1919 Fame and Fortune Contest and the April 1919 cover of *Motion Picture Classic*. During a summer trip to New York City, a "well-known movie actor" secured some background work for the budding thespian at Vitagraph; her hunger for screen work continued long after she returned to Davenport. After one more year of both academic and dramatic studies, she toured the Midwest with a traveling stock company and was active in the community-based Little Theatre Movement. In 1921, her wavy brown hair, hazel eyes, and "poise and grace of one years older" charmed the *Chicago Tribune* into awarding her $1000 and the title of the "prettiest girl in Iowa." Official movie roles followed, the first being as a maid in *Penrod* (1922), based on Tarkington's comedic stories and directed by Marshall Neilan. She was voted "Miss Hollywood" by her peers in 1923, appearing at functions and sculpted by Finn Haaken Frolich. Her career exploded after the ultimate validation: a spot on the 1924 WAMPAS Baby Star roster (the same year as Clara Bow), and roles were plentiful. She frequently appeared in comedies and in Westerns alongside Fred Thompson, but her most iconic role was "The College Belle" in Harold Lloyd's *The Freshman* (1925). Her roles dwindled in frequency and importance as the years progressed, but she remained on screens both big and small until 1966, opposite everyone from Barbara La Marr and Harry Langdon to Loretta Young and William "Hopalong Cassidy" Boyd. Keener married twice, the first to actor Francis Smith in 1922 (over, perhaps annulled, by 1923), the second to salesman Ross Chatelain in 1932.

By the mid-1970s, in the last years of her life, she was a minister at the Ventura County Church of Religious Science. Hazel Ona Keener died of cardiac arrest in August 1979, two months shy of her 75th birthday.

### MARY NOLAN

Mary Imogene Robertson was born in Kentucky and moved to NY as a teenager. While modeling, her exceptional beauty caught Florenz Ziegfeld's eye and he fatefully cast her in his *Follies*. Under the stage name Imogene "Bubbles" Wilson, she became their most popular dancer—and the mistress of *Follies* headliner Frank Tinney. Their relationship was violent, and when one of Tinney's beatings left her hospitalized, the resulting press ruined the comedian's career and got Wilson fired. She fled to Germany and made movies there until Universal signed her to a Hollywood contract in 1927. This, as you could imagine, raised a lot of eyebrows:

"In view of the motion picture industry's attitude towards Corliss Palmer and the amazing coldness of producers towards Peaches Browning... the signing of Miss Wilson is causing comment."

Wilson, rechristened Mary Nolan, surprised the tongue-waggers by giving intelligent, nuanced performances opposite such greats as John Gilbert and Lon Chaney Sr. For a brief time, she was sought after, successful, completely reinvented. Then came another affair, this time with notorious MGM fixer Eddie Mannix, who also beat her terribly and forced her to have an abortion on at least one occasion. After news of their affair leaked, Mannix and MGM publicity head Howard Strickling mounted a smear campaign against her; this, combined with drug abuse and combative on-set behavior, spelled her end in movies. After a few low-budget roles and a short-lived marriage, she moved to New York to attempt a nightclub cabaret act. It didn't take off and she was back in Hollywood by 1939, the rest of her life a haze of addiction, arrests, and poor health. Police found Nolan's severely malnourished body in her apartment on October 31, 1948; cause of death was cardiac arrest, liver disease, and an overdose of barbiturates. Whether it was intentional remained her secret. Nolan, the "hard-luck girl," was only 42.

# CLOSING CREDITS

*Have you ever paused to consider into what unknown limbo the plays and players of yesteryear have gone?*

*– Motion Picture*, July 1920

**ELEANOR** never remarried. She lived with **VIRGIL** in upstate New York, then New Jersey, where she dabbled in real estate and he in run-ins with the law; in 1959 he pled guilty to a gun charge and received an eleven-month suspended sentence. Eleanor died in NJ on March 14, 1953.

**EMILIE** also never remarried. She enjoyed her eclectic interests until her death in Michigan on May 10, 1947. **RUTH** had a son and daughter, and died in Florida on Oct 6, 1976. **RAFAEL** eloped in 1923 with Hazel Spyr, and they had a son and daughter together. In 1947 Hazel sued Raphael for divorce, charging he'd "neglected her for 15 years, been enamored of other women, and absent from home for long periods." (Apple, tree, etc.) He died in Florida on August 30, 1979. **MARIE THERESA** was a kindergarten teacher before marrying childhood sweetheart Kenneth Lane in 1932. Later, the two worked in real estate down in Florida. She died only four days after her husband, on February 17, 1969.

**LIANE** created the short-lived Gotham Literary Circle in 1939, a project she and Brewster started before his death, to find and promote "new writers of unusual promise." She co-wrote a novel in 1941, *Year by Candlelight*, about a Brooklyn writer involved with a movie producer who'd lost four wives and his entire fortune. (Really, folks, there are other plots!) The

111

*New York Times* review: "pretentious awkwardness." By the 1950s she'd taken over the Hotel Garde in Hartford, Connecticut, and reinvented herself as a specialist in "taking low-producing properties and making them pay off." In the mid-1950s she remarried and moved to Miami, FL.

**JULIA SR.** stayed in California, listing herself as Luther's widow for the rest of her life. She died in Los Angeles in 1967. **MARY** and **ENNIS** were her only children to outlive her; Mary died in 1969, Ennis in 1989, both in California. **JAMES CALVIN** served under Patton in WWII. He was married at the time of his death in 1960. **KATHERINE** married Albert Frederickson, a driver for RKO. When daughter Christine, raised in the studio's shadow, expressed a desire to go into movies, Kay's reply was: "We DON'T want an actress in this family!". She and Al were married 68 years and moved to Arizona after his retirement.

**JULIA JR.** was an enigma. Katherine once told her daughter about a sister arrested for theft, who died in prison. A letter Julia Jr. wrote to Katherine in the late 1930s asserts: "I don't believe you will ever find me so don't try. You all seem to think I'm a criminal… well, you were halfway right." She ended by promising to visit Mom someday; in 1946 The *Central New Jersey Home News* reports a "Julia Simone" of Glendale, CA was sentenced to the Women's Reformatory at Clinton (now the Edna Mahan Correctional Facility for Women) for public lewdness. She deserves a book of her own!

**WILLIAM TAYLOR** remained in Glendale after Corliss' death, and in 1953 was a maintenance man in a local bowling alley. Nothing further after this—just too many William Taylors to be definitive.

**WILLIAM RICHARD MIDDLETON** married in 1936, had two children, and got a great job in Florida as territory manager for Ford. He died in 1976.

**LILLIAN MONTANYE** died in 1930. **FREDERICK J.** and **AGNES SMITH** continued editing, reviewing and writing about film for various publications until their respective (and untimely) deaths in 1933 and 1941.

**AL AND JEANNE COHEN** had two daughters, actress Louise Sorel and actress/charity fundraiser Mishka Minchon. In addition to assorted film and TV roles like *Prehistoric Women* (1950) and Mrs. Vandersnoot in the 1967 Christmas episode of *The Monkees*, Jeanne founded and taught at the Oxford Theatre in Los Angeles. She died in 2003. Al produced at Republic and Universal, then wrote and produced for TV, notably *The Ann Southern Show* (1958-1961). He died in 1984.

Deep within the Normandy Park Historic District of Morris Township, NJ is the last vestige of **CHERRYCROFT**, the carriage house, converted to a residence in the 1980s. A 2016 real estate listing points out "a pond, rare specimen trees and shrubs, benches and stone slabs," remnants of the original estate. Also within the district is **ELEVEN OAKS**, still intact. It was featured in a 2006 episode of *The Sopranos*.

*MOTION PICTURE CLASSIC* ceased publication in 1931. By 1941, *MOTION PICTURE* merged with two other fan magazines, *Hollywood* and *Screen Life*. The final issue, with Natalie Wood on the cover, was published in December 1977.

# BIBLIOGRAPHY

"California Death Index, 1940-1997," database, FamilySearch (https://familysearch. org/ark:/61903/1:1:VPCQ-J9Q : 26 November 2014), Hazel Ona Keener, 07 Aug 1979; Department of Public Health Services, Sacramento.

"California, County Marriages, 1850-1952," database with images, FamilySearch (https://familysearch.org/ark:/61903/1:1:K8JS-CNG : 31 July 2017), Eugene V Brewster and Corliss Modena Palmer, 19 Mar 1931; citing Los Angeles, California, United States, county courthouses, California; FHL microfilm 2,074,885.

"California, County Marriages, 1850-1952," database with images, FamilySearch (https://familysearch.org/ark:/61903/1:1:K88M-Y9F : 5 August 2017), Francis H Smith and Hazel O Keener, 11 Jan 1922; citing Los Angeles, California, United States, county courthouses, California; FHL microfilm 2,074,274.

"Florida Death Index, 1877-1998," database, FamilySearch (https://familysearch.org/ ark:/61903/1:1:VVQJ-6CF : 25 December 2014), Ruth Dobie, 06 Oct 1976; from "Florida Death Index, 1877-1998," index, Ancestry (www.ancestry. com : 2004); citing vol. , certificate number 71030, Florida Department of Health, Office of Vital Records, Jacksonville.

"Florida Death Index, 1877-1998," database, FamilySearch (https://familysearch.org/ ark:/61903/1:1:VVQ8-WHF : 25 December 2014), Rafael Churbuck Brewster, 30 Aug 1979; from "Florida Death Index, 1877-1998," index, Ancestry (www.ancestry.com : 2004); citing vol. , certificate number 65635, Florida Department of Health, Office of Vital Records, Jacksonville.

"New York, New York City Municipal Deaths, 1795-1949," database, FamilySearch (https://familysearch.org/ark:/61903/1:1:2WVT-R2D : 20 March 2015), Lilly De La Montanye, 31 Jul 1930; citing Death, Brooklyn, Kings, New York, United States, New York Municipal Archives, New York; FHL microfilm 2,069,169.

"Tennessee, County Marriages, 1790-1950," database with images, FamilySearch (https://familysearch.org/ark:/61903/1:1:QKHQ-15VP : 14 October 2017), Ralph William Cain and Florine F De Hart, 17 Sep 1927; citing Sullivan, Tennessee, United States, Marriage, p. , Tennessee State Library and Archives, Nashville and county clerk offices from various counties; FHL microfilm 1,928,834.

"United States Census, 1900," database with images, FamilySearch (https://family-search.org/ark:/61903/1:1:MSNC-DTG : accessed 23 July 2016), Eugene V Brewster, Borough of Brooklyn, Election District 12 New York City Ward 23, Kings, New York, United States; citing enumeration district (ED) 392, sheet 19A, family 431, NARA microfilm publication T623 (Washington, D.C.: National Archives and Records Administration, 1972.); FHL micro-film 1,241,061.

"United States Census, 1900," database with images, FamilySearch (https://familyse-arch.org/ark:/61903/1:1:M3FG-NDS : accessed 23 July 2016), Helen Palm-er in household of Luther Palmer, Militia District Quitman town, Brooks, Georgia, United States; citing enumeration district (ED) 6, sheet 16A, fam-ily 296, NARA microfilm publication T623 (Washington, D.C.: National Archives and Records Administration, 1972.); FHL microfilm 1,240,181.

"$200,000 for Her Broken Heart—Collected—One Fur Coat." *The Indianapolis Star* (IN), January 2, 1927.

"'Broadway Fever'—with Sally O'Neill [sic]." Review. *Harrison's Reports*, February 16, 1929.

"'Corliss Palmer' in San Francisco Jail." *Nevada State Journal*, February 1, 1933.

"'Divorce or No Divorce, I Will Never Leave Eugene,' Corliss States." *Oakland Tri-bune* (CA), April 5, 1924.

"'Georgia Peach' of Films Sued for Large Sum." *The Nevada State Journal*, September 22, 1932.

"'Red Kisses' At Gayety is Diamond Camp Drama." *The St. Louis Star and Times* (MO), March 7, 1927.

"'The Night Bird'—With Reginald Denny." Review. *Harrison's Reports*, September 8, 1928.

"A $250,000 Wedding Gift—But No Wedding Ring." *The Ogden Standard-Examiner* (UT), February 24, 1924.

"A New Brewster Publication." *Advertising and Selling*, November 12, 1921.

"A Picture That Has Great Appeal." *The Film Spectator*, January 21, 1928.

"A Typical Finish." *Detroit Free Press*, February 2, 1933.

"Actress in Outbreak." *Los Angeles Times*, February 1, 1933.

"Actress Sure She Can Hold Love of Millionaire Brewster." *The Washington Times* (DC), December 6, 1922.

"Actress to Charge Mate With Neglect." *Ironwood Daily Globe* (MI), August 6, 1933.

"Agnes Ayres in 'Into the Night.'" Review. *Film Daily*, August 26, 1928.

"Agnes Egan Cobb Signs Palmer Pictures." *Motion Picture News*, August 5, 1922.

"Alienation Charged." *The Pantagraph* (Bloomington, IL), September 22, 1932.

"Allene Ray and Larry Wheeler Married." *Motion Picture News*, August 8, 1925.

"Allene Ray." *IMDb: The Internet Movie Database*. Web. Accessed February 4, 2017. (http://www.imdb.com/name/nm0712735)

"Anna V. Hervey." Obituary. *New York Times*, March 18, 1922.

"Another Bad Slip in Corliss Palmer's Path." *Variety,* February 7, 1933.

"Another Southern Beauty Selected By Brewster." *Brooklyn Daily Eagle* (NY), June 8, 1923.

"At the Egyptian: Charm and Comedy Abound in New Dowling Hit." *The Park Record* (Park City, UT), August 14, 1931.

"At the Rivoli." *The Baltimore Sun*, February 28, 1932.

"Beauty Accused of Love Theft in $100,000 Suit." *The San Bernardino County Sun* (CA), September 22, 1932.

"Beauty Divorced." *The Mansfield News-Journal* (OH), December 8, 1933.

"Beauty Winner Is In Hospital." *Reno Evening Gazette* (NV), February 1, 1933.

"Biographical Note." *Papers of Albert J. Cohen*, The University of Iowa Libraries, Iowa City, IA. Web. Accessed June 17, 2016. (https://www.lib.uiowa.edu/scua/ msc/tomsc150/msc126/msc126.htm)

"Bisque Dolls Are His Best Sellers." *Santa Cruz Evening News* (CA), December 10, 1927.

"Blackton, Pioneer in Movies, Dies, 66." *New York Times,* August 14, 1941.

"Blames Film Actress in Separation Suit." *New York Times*, December 2, 1922.

"Blanche Bates." *IMDb: The Internet Movie Database*. Web. Accessed March 19, 2017. (http://www.imdb.com/name/nm0060857)

"Blocking the Romances of the Hat-Check Girls." *Oakland Tribune* (CA), September 12, 1937.

"Brewster 'Threw' Fan Magazines to Film Co." *Variety*, May 26, 1926.

"Brewster as Agent." *Variety,* March 29, 1932.

"Brewster as Book Publisher." *Variety,* June 7, 1932.

"Brewster Assets Transferred, Wife Blocked, He Says." *Brooklyn Daily Eagle* (NY), November 24, 1926.

"Brewster Attachment No Good." *The Southeast Missourian*, November 24, 1926.

"Brewster Creditor Claims Control of Movie Magazines." *Brooklyn Daily Eagle* (NY), November 9, 1926.

"Brewster Brothers' Death 3 Days Apart." *Variety*, January 11, 1939.

"Brewster Deserts Beauty." *Los Angeles Times*, June 25, 1926.

"Brewster Hunts New Riches for 4th Wife." *Brooklyn Daily Eagle* (NY), April 16, 1932.

"Brewster Is 'Broke,' Corliss to Act Again." *Milwaukee Journal* (WI), August 7, 1931.

"Brewster is Back, Seeking His Millions." *Brooklyn Daily Eagle* (NY), January 5, 1934.

"Brewster Kept Charm While Losing Millions." *Brooklyn Daily Eagle* (NY), January 8, 1939.

"Brewster Magazines Announce Winners of 'The Fame and Fortune Contest.'" *Moving Picture World*, November 20, 1920.

"Brewster on Brewster." *Variety*, October 12, 1927.

"Brewster Sacrifices Art." *New York Times*, December 11, 1927.

"Brewster Selling Home." *Variety*, July 13, 1927.

"Brewster Sponsors Modest Productions." *Exhibitors Herald*, February 19, 1921.

"Brewster to Wed Beautiful Singer." *Modesto News-Herald* (CA), April 11, 1932.

"Brewster Weds Again." *San Antonio Express* (TX), March 25, 1935.

"Brewster Will Not Finance Corliss' Movie Aspirations." *Brooklyn Daily Eagle* (NY), January 29, 1926.

"Brewster, 'Great Lover,' Through With Women Forever." *Milwaukee Journal* (WI), November 17, 1934.

"Brewster, Once Glorifier of Beauty, Sees New Fortune in Tooth Paste [sic]." *Brooklyn Daily Eagle* (NY), July 17, 1934.

"Brewster's 'Face-Lift.'" *Variety*, July 14, 1926.

"Brewster's Auction Sale $50,000 Under Program." *Variety*, December 21, 1927.

"Brewster's Daughter Upholds His Stand." *Detroit Free Press*, December 8, 1922.

"Brewster's Land Asked in Bank Suit." *Los Angeles Times*, January 12, 1932.

"Brewster's Love Nest for Corliss Palmer Sold to Schwab's Brother for $90,000." *The Bridgeport Telegram* (CT), August 10, 1926.

"Brewster's Millions Almost Back." *New York Post*, July 31, 1936.

"Brewster-Palmer Love Difficulty In Court Today." *Atlanta Constitution* (GA), December 4, 1922.

"Broadway Fever." Review. *Film Daily*, February 17, 1929.

"Broadway Fever." Review. *Film Daily*, January 6, 1929.

"Brother of Movie Star Electrocuted." *The Greenville News* (SC), July 26, 1936.

"Calls Love Triangle 'Fanciful Goulash.'" *The Washington Herald* (DC), December 5, 1922.

"Carleton Brewster Dies." *Motion Picture Herald*, January 7, 1939.

"Cast Member: Wilna Webster Hervey." *The Three Stooges Online Filmography*. Web. Accessed August 3, 2017. (http://threestooges.net/cast/actor/4071)

"Casting New Faces." *New York Times*, July 8, 1923.

"Causing Comment." *The Nebraska State Journal*, March 13, 1927.

"Clip and Paste." *The Moving Picture World*, April 3, 1920.

"Clothes Make the Woman." Review. *Film Daily*, June 24, 1928.

"Code of Divorce Etiquette is Formulated by Mrs. Brewster No. 1 Through Scientific Prayer." *The Evening Public Ledger* (Philadelphia, PA), December 12, 1922.

"Concert By Italian Conservatory of Music." *Brooklyn Daily Eagle* (NY), May 8, 1910.

"Contest Brings Deluge of Beauty." *Motion Picture*, March 1921.

"Contest Resumé." *Motion Picture*, February 1921.

"Corless [sic] Now Quite Happy." *The Herald Democrat* (Leadville, CO), December 25, 1922.

"Corliss Again Named in Suit." *The Maryville Tribune* (OH), September 22, 1932.

"Corliss At Hollywood Home Again." *Los Angeles Times*, April 7, 1933.

"Corliss Has A Bout With Death." *The Indiana Gazette* (Indiana, PA), February 2, 1933.

"Corliss Must Answer." *Variety*, August 18, 1926.

"Corliss Palmer and her Hubby Will Separate." *Sarasota Herald-Tribune* (FL), October 21, 1931.

"Corliss Palmer Begins Her Climb to Stardom." *Moving Picture World*, March 19, 1921.

"Corliss Palmer Feels Work of Moral Benefit." *Los Angeles Times*, February 19, 1928.

"Corliss Palmer Granted Divorce From Brewster." *The Lincoln Star* (NE), December 5, 1933.

"Corliss Palmer Ill in San Francisco Hospital With 'Chronic Alcoholism.'" *Brooklyn Daily Eagle* (NY), February 1, 1933.

"Corliss Palmer In 'Trial Marriage' At The Majestic." *Hartford Courant* (CT), February 17, 1929.

"Corliss Palmer in Fist Fight With Her Rival." *St. Petersburg Times* (FL), February 2, 1933.

"Corliss Palmer Is Alcohol Case." *Asbury Park Press* (NJ), February 1, 1933.

"Corliss Palmer Is Cheered By Notes." *Modesto News-Herald* (CA), February 3, 1933.

"Corliss Palmer is Forcibly Taken to Hospital on Coast." *Wausau Daily Herald* (WI), February 1, 1933.

"Corliss Palmer Is In Franklin Film." *Oakland Tribune* (CA), August 25, 1928.

"Corliss Palmer Is Not Allowed Guests." *The San Bernardino County Sun* (CA), February 3, 1933

"Corliss Palmer is Sued." *New York Times,* September 22, 1932.

"Corliss Palmer Leaves Hospital." *The New York Sun,* February 7, 1933.

"Corliss Palmer May Be Club's Hostess." *The San Bernardino County Sun* (CA), February 9, 1933.

"Corliss Palmer Plans To Divorce Brewster." *Brooklyn Daily Eagle* (NY), April 8, 1933.

"Corliss Palmer Recovers." *Harrisburg Telegraph* (PA), February 2, 1933.

"Corliss Palmer Recovers; Sends for Hollywood Writer." *Brooklyn Daily Eagle* (NY), February 2, 1933.

"Corliss Palmer Replies." *New York Times,* September 23, 1932.

"Corliss Palmer Sues Writer." *New York Times,* August 12, 1933.

"Corliss Palmer to Model Gowns Here." *Arizona Daily Star,* October 8, 1935.

"Corliss Palmer Weds Brewster in Mexico." *New York Times,* October 30, 1926.

"Corliss Palmer Will Ask Divorce From Magazine Publisher." *The News-Herald* (Franklin, PA), August 25, 1933.

"Corliss Palmer, Corespondent [sic] in Brewster Suit, Writes About the Perfect Woman; Edits Beauty Box." *Brooklyn Daily Eagle* (NY), December 3, 1922.

"Corliss Palmer." *IMDb: The Internet Movie Database.* Web. Accessed December 27, 2016. (http://www.imdb.com/name/nm0658176)

"Corliss Palmer's Brother Killed By Electric Wire." *The Butler Herald* (GA), July 20, 1936.

"Corliss Palmer's Name." *Variety,* June 16, 1926.

"Corliss Palmer's Name." *Variety,* May 23, 1928.

"Corliss Palmer's Sister Vanishes." *The Minneapolis Star* (MN), July 3, 1926.

"Corliss Palmer's Sweetie Enraged When He Learns of Her Liking for Brewster." *San Antonio Evening News* (TX), December 15, 1922.

"Corliss Played at Love, Says Former Swain." *The Washington Herald* (DC), December 13, 1922.

"Corliss Still Lives Home At Morristown; 1,000-Mile Jaunt Story is a Mystery." *Brooklyn Daily Eagle* (NY), March 4, 1924.

"Corliss Sues Former Wooer." *The Pittsburg Press* (PA), August 11, 1933.

"Corliss, You'd Better Lock Up Your Things." *Milwaukee Sentinel* (WI), March 13, 1926.

"Costly Brewster Bric-a-Brac Auctioned Off Away Under Par." *The Miami News* (FL), December 10, 1927.

"Court Waiting for Defendant in Beauty Suit." *The Evening Independent* (St. Petersburg, FL), March 6, 1926.

"Crazed Woman May Be Corliss Palmer." *The Courier-Journal* (Louisville, KY), February 1, 1933.

"Curious Dilemma of Love-Robbed Mrs. Brewster." *The Courier-Journal* (Louisville, KY), April 11, 1926.

"Dam-Break Scenic Shown at Tally's." *Los Angeles Times*, March 20, 1928.

"Dear Mr. Brewster Picks Another Prize Beauty." *The Pittsburg Press* (PA), July 15, 1923.

"Death Data Sought By Corliss Palmer." *Los Angeles Times*, July 26, 1931.

"Divorce Won by Wife of Manufacturer." *Detroit Free Press*, November 29, 1947.

"Divorced Wife of Millionaire Gets $50,000." *Albuquerque Journal* (NM), November 23, 1926.

"Dr. Jacob Casson "Jake" Geiger." *FindAGrave*. Web. Accessed April 12, 2017. (https://www.findagrave.com/cgi-bin/fg.cgi?page=gr&GRid= 91151223)

"Dream of 'Miss America' Is Ended After Five Years." *Pittsburg Post-Gazette* (PA), March 8, 1930.

"Driver Fined $15 On Two Charges." *Star-Gazette* (Elmira, NY), July 11, 1949.

"E. Mason Hopper to Direct 'Up in Mabel's Room.'" *Motion Picture News*, March 27, 1926.

"E.V. Brewster to Bring Religion to Broadway." *Brooklyn Daily Eagle* (NY), November 22, 1936.

"E.V. Brewster Weds Quietly in Jersey." *New York Times,* March 24, 1935.

"E.V. Brewster Wins Bride in Rockaway." *Brooklyn Daily Eagle* (NY), January 3, 1917.

"E.V. Brewster's Widow Organizes New Authors' Club." *Brooklyn Daily Eagle* (NY), October 8, 1939.

"Eldora E. Ferrell." *FindAGrave*. Web. Accessed April 12, 2017. (https://www.findagrave.com/cgi-bin/fg.cgi?page=gr&GRid= 88911295)

"Elva Pomfret." *IBDb: The Internet Broadway Database*. Web. Accessed April 24, 2017. (https://www.ibdb.com/broadway-cast-staff/elva-pomfret-115288)

"Ennis Didn't Get Much Of A Prize At That." *The Batavia Times* (NY), July 10, 1926.

"Erminie Gagnon." *IMDb: The Internet Movie Database*. Web. Accessed January 9, 2017. (http://www.imdb.com/name/nm0300975)

"Eugene Brewster Funeral Rites Held." *Brooklyn Daily Eagle* (NY), January 3, 1939.

"Eugene Brewster is Dead." *The Nebraska State Journal* (Lincoln, NE), January 2, 1939.

"Eugene Brewster, Publisher, Dies." *Motion Picture Herald*, January 7, 1939.

"Eugene Brewster, Publisher, Was 67." *New York Times*, January 2, 1939.

"Eugene Brewster's Condition Unchanged." *Brooklyn Daily Eagle* (NY), December 31, 1938.

"Eugene V. Brewster." *askArt*. Web. Accessed January 27, 2016. (http://www.askart.com/artist/Eugene_V_Brewster/10006493/Eugene_V_Brewster.aspx)

"Eugene V. Brewster." *Successful American*, September 1902.

"Eugene V. Brewster's Son Elopes With Hazel Spur." *Brooklyn Daily Eagle* (NY), August 2, 1923.

"Ex-Beauty Champion Remarries." *Los Angeles Times*, July 21, 1931.

"Ex-Millionaire Loses His Home; Has Hopes Left." *The Argus-Leader* (Sioux Falls, SD), January 12, 1932.

"Ex-Movie Actress Now Hospital Case." *Ludington Daily News* (MI), February 1, 1933.

"Fashion News (1930)." *IMDb: The Internet Movie Database*. Web. Accessed March 22, 2017. (http://www.imdb.com/title/tt1410233)

"Fay Lanphier Grows Shy, Dodges Divorce Audience." *Oakland Tribune* (CA), March 9, 1929.

"Fay Lanphier." *IMDb: The Internet Movie Database*. Web. Accessed May 3, 2017. (http://www.imdb.com/name/nm0487035/)

"Florence Vidor in 'Honeymoon Hate.'" Review. *Film Daily*, December 25, 1927.

"Former Suitor of Corliss 'Bereft.'" *The Washington Times* (DC), December 8, 1922.

"Freezing Out Corliss Palmer; No One Wants Home Wrecker." *Variety*, March 10, 1926.

"General Denials in Love Suits." *The Zanesville Signal* (OH), October 5, 1932.

"George Washington Cohen." Review. *Film Daily*, May 19, 1929.

"Georgia Peach Again Models." *San Bernardino Sun* (CA), October 12, 1935.

"Georgia Peach of Film Fame Sues Ex-Lover." *The Evening News* (Wilkes-Barre, PA), August 12, 1933.

"Ghostly Belva Barks at Bara." *Photoplay*, May 1917.

"Good Things A-Coming for 1918." *Motion Picture*, December 1917.

"Grady Watterson Palmer." *FindAGrave*. Web. Accessed April 12, 2017. (https://www.findagrave.com/cgi-bin/fg.cgi?page=gr&GRid= 62660334)

"Hazel Keener Chosen Queen of Hollywood." *Quad-City Times* (Davenport, IA), May 27, 1923.

"Hazel Keener." *IMDb: The Internet Movie Database*. Web. Accessed September 14, 2017. (http://www.imdb.com/name/nm0444753)

"Himmel + Meringoff Announces Renovation of 729 Seventh Avenue in Midtown West MdeAS Architects Retained in the Re-Design." *Citybizlist*, September 16, 2015. Web. Accessed Feb 19, 2016. (http://citybizlist.com/article/299821/himmel-meringoff-announces-renovation-of-729-seventh-avenue-in-midtown-west-mdeas-architects-retained-in-the-re-design)

"History." *Masonic Home of Georgia*. Web. Accessed 01-20-2016. (http://masonichomeofgeorgia.com/History/History.html)

"Honeymoon Hate—Paramount." Review. *Photoplay*, January 1928.

"I Chased the Rainbow—and Now Look At Me!" *Portsmouth Daily Times* (OH), March 12, 1933.

"In the Wings." *Brooklyn Daily Eagle* (NY), November 30, 1936.

"Incorporations." *Film Daily*, March 2, 1921.

"Inside Stuff—Pictures." *Variety*, September 5, 1933.

"International Beauty of 1922 Sets Out to Make Comeback." *The Racine Journal-Times* (WI), October 9, 1935.

"Into the Night." Review. *Film Daily*, August 26, 1928.

"James Palmer." Obituary. *The Van Nuys News* (CA), April 19, 1960.

"Jeanne Sorel Cohen." Obituary. *Variety.com*, January 28, 2003. Web. Accessed March 3, 2017. http://variety.com/2003/scene/people-news/jeanne-sorel-cohen-1117879636/

"Jeanne Sorel." *IMDb: The Internet Movie Database*. Web. Accessed May 8, 2016. (http://www.imdb.com/name/nm0814801)

"Jemison's History." *Official Website for the City of Jemison*. Web. Accessed September 13, 2017. (http://www.jemisonalabama.org/about/jemisons-history/)

"Jules Brulatour Dies at 76 in New York; Pioneer of Film Biz." *Variety*, October 23, 1946.

"Julia Alma Farrell Palmer." *FindAGrave*. Web. Accessed April 12, 2017. (https://www.findagrave.com/cgi-bin/fg.cgi?page=gr&GRid=154293342)

"Just One Love Tangle After Another!" *Portsmouth Daily Times* (OH), October 23, 1932.

"Kathryn McGuire." *IMDb: The Internet Movie Database*. Web. Accessed March 20, 2017. (http://www.imdb.com/name/nm0570230/)

"LeBaron Welcomed in Hollywood." *Motion Picture News*, June 17, 1927.

"Leonora von Ottinger." *IMDb: The Internet Movie Database*. Web. Accessed March 20, 2017. (http://www.imdb.com/name/nm0902785)

"lightningbrice," "Getwell, Anetha." *An Encyclopedia of Obscure Silent Screen Performers*, May 19, 2016. Web. Accessed May 9, 2017. (https://theencyclopediaofobscuresilentscreenperformers.wordpress.com/2016/05/19/getwell-anetha)

"Long Estate Wrangle Ends." *Star-Gazette* (Elmira, NY), October 16, 1947.

"Louise Sorel." *IMDb: The Internet Movie Database*. Web. Accessed May 8, 2016. (http://www.imdb.com/name/nm0814798)

"Love's Redemption (1921)." *IMDb: The Internet Movie Database*. Web. Accessed February 4, 2017. (http://www.imdb.com/title/tt0333835)

"Macon Has the Most Beautiful Girl in America." *The Newnan Herald* (GA), October 29, 1920.

"Man Fined $100 In Gun Case." *The Courier-News* (Bridgewater, NJ), October 24, 1959.

"Married Admirer Her Only Real Love, Vows Prize Beauty." *Philadelphia Inquirer*, December 10, 1922.

"Mary Nolan." *IMDb: The Internet Movie Database*. Web. Accessed September 2, 2017. (http://www.imdb.com/name/nm0634322)

"Mildred Bowling." Obituary. *The Baltimore Sun*, August 14, 1922.

"Mildred K. Bowling." *FindAGrave*. Web. Accessed April 12, 2017. (https://www.findagrave.com/cgi-bin/fg.cgi?page=gr&GRid=82899573)

"Most Beautiful Girl in America." *The Home Journal* (Perry, GA), October 25, 1920.

"Motion Picture Magazine Again Changes Owners." *Hartford Courant* (CT), June 16, 1937.

"Movie Beauty Moved to General Hospital." *The Ogden Standard-Examiner* (UT), February 3, 1933.

"Mr. Brewster An Editor." *Brooklyn Daily Eagle* (NY), January 10, 1909.

"Mr. Brewster's 'Incurable Smattering' That Cost Him 3 Wives, 3 Millions." *The San Antonio Light* (TX), February 5, 1939.

"Mr. Brewster's Newest 'Dearest Girl on Earth' Romance, No.5." *Philadelphia Inquirer*, May 15, 1932.

"Mr. Kenneth Lane." Obituary. *The Orlando Sentinel* (FL), February 14, 1969.

"Mr. M.L. Palmer Died." *Quitman Advertiser* (GA), June 24, 1910.

"Mrs. Brewster Sues Corliss For $400,000 as Love Nest Furnishings Sell for Song." *Brooklyn Daily Eagle* (NY), April 5, 1924.

"Mrs. Brewster Wins Legal Victory." *Variety*, July 28, 1926.

"Mrs. Brewster's $200,000 Love Suit Fails to Worry Corliss; Brewster Defiant." *Brooklyn Daily Eagle* (NY), April 6, 1924.

"Mrs. Eleanor V.V. Brewster." Obituary. *The Elmira Advertiser* (NY), March 16, 1953.

"Mrs. Marie B. Lane." Obituary. *The Orlando Sentinel* (FL), February 18, 1969.

"New Cast Names at Belmont to Draw on Films." *Los Angeles Times,* April 5, 1927.

"New Names in Who's Who." *Brooklyn Daily Eagle* (NY), October 13, 1936.

"New Pictures: 'Polly of the Movies.'" *Exhibitors Herald and Moving Picture World*, January 7,1928.

"New Romance for Brewster is Reported." *New Castle News* (PA), April 16, 1932.

"News Flash." *Brooklyn Daily Eagle* (NY), November 16, 1936.

"News From the Dailies." *Variety*, August 15, 1933.

"No Longer a Feast." *The Pittsburg Press* (PA), March 24, 1889.

"Official Warns All Exhibitors." *Variety*, August 24, 1927.

"Old-Timers Now Gladly Play 'Bits.'" *Hartford Courant* (CT), October 28, 1934.

"Omnibus of Crime." *Variety*, September 16, 1936.

"Once Millionaire Sued for Property." *Oakland Tribune* (CA), January 12, 1932.

"Peggy Wood." *IMDb: The Internet Movie Database.* Web. Accessed March 20, 2017. (http://www.imdb.com/name/nm0939931)

"Philanthropic Experiment With Georgia News-Stand Girl Ends in Domestic Disaster." *St. Louis Post-Dispatch* (MS), December 10, 1922.

"Picture Brides (1934)." *IMDb: The Internet Movie Database.* Web. Accessed May 8, 2016. (http://www.imdb.com/title/tt0024449)

"Picture Brides." Capsule review. *Photoplay*, April 1934.

"Picture Brides." Review. *Photoplay*, December 1933.

"Picture Plays and People." *New York Times*, November 13, 1921.

"Plays Out of Town: 'Red Kisses.'" *Variety*, April 20, 1927.

"Pretty Clerk Denies She Vamped Rich Man." *Detroit Free Press*, December 4, 1922.

"Public Opinion Kills Romance of Publisher." *The San Bernardino County Sun* (CA), March 15, 1924.

"Raymond J and Elva Pomfret Nagle Associate Professor of Restorative Dentistry and Biomaterials Sciences." *Harvard Catalyst Profiles*. Web. Accessed April 24, 2017. (https://connects.catalyst.harvard.edu/Profiles/display/64697073)

"Reginald Denny in 'The Night Bird.'" Review. *Film Daily*, October 7, 1928.

"Rialto Gossip." *New York Times*, April 19, 1936.

"Richard Barthelmess in 'The Noose.'" Review. *Film Daily*, January 15, 1928.

"Rolph Pardons Much-Publicized Movie Producer." *Nevada State Journal*, December 28, 1933.

"Romance Ended." *The Lincoln Star* (NE), December 12, 1933.

"Romance of Beauty Ends in Hollywood." *The Palm Beach Post* (FL), October 12, 1931.

"Says His Romance With 'Georgia Peach' Is Ended." *The Garrett Clipper* (IN), October 15, 1931.

"Scarlet Youth." Review. *Photoplay*, April 1928.

"Screen Role Won by Russian Beauty." *Los Angeles Times*, April 4, 1932.

"Selected 'Most Beautiful Girl in America.'" *Asbury Park Press* (NJ), May 7, 1923.

"Sex Film at Tally's in Eighth Week." *Los Angeles Times,* March 11, 1928.

"Sex Films Are Lucrative." *Philadelphia Inquirer* (PA), August 26, 1937.

"She Vamped Him for Six Years, Declares Richard Middleton, Giving Out Corliss Palmer Love Letters." *Des Moines Tribune* (IA), December 14, 1922.

"Short Subjects: 'Bromo and Juliet'—Hal Roach—Pathé—Fine Laughmaker." *Film Daily*, September 12, 1926.

"Simone Seeks Reconciliation With His Wife." *Atlanta Constitution* (GA), December 6, 1922.

"Sint Millard, Once Host to Queen, Fights Jail Term." *Oakland Tribune* (CA), June 25, 1928.

"Society: Rotary Anns Are Entertained." *Kingsport Times* (TN), April 22, 1930.

"Stanton Palmer." *FindAGrave*. Web. Accessed April 12, 2017. (https://www.findagrave.com/cgi-bin/fg.cgi?page=gr&GRid= 135982782)

"Sues For Alleged $50 Publicity Fee." *The Ogden Standard Examiner* (UT), November 23, 1927.

"Suit in Filmdom Brings Results." *Pittsburg Post-Gazette* (PA), August 12, 1933.

"Tells of Thwarted Love." *St. Petersburg Times* (FL), February 2, 1933.

"The Answer Man." *Motion Picture*, July 1921.

"The Film Estimates: Clothes Make the Woman." Review. *The Educational Screen*, October 1928.

"The Film Estimates: George Washington Cohen." Review. *The Educational Screen*, June 1929.

"The House of Gloria's Dreams." *Picture-Play*, May 1923.

"The Night Bird." Review. *Exhibitors Herald-World*, July 20, 1929.

"The Night Bird." Review. *Harrison's Reports*, September 8, 1928.

"The Night Bird." Review. *Variety*, October 3, 1928.

"The Noose." Review. *Film Daily*, January 15, 1928.

"The Noose." Review. *Film Daily*, January 3, 1928.

"The Noose." Review. *Variety,* March 21, 1928.

"The Princess Pola's Chateau." *Picture Play*, November 1927.

"The Promise Fulfilled." *Motion Picture Classic*, October 1923.

"The Return of Boston Blackie." Review. *Film Daily*, September 18, 1927.

"The Shadow Stage: Honeymoon Lane." Review. *Photoplay,* September 1931.

"The Shadow Stage: Polly of the Movies." Review. *Photoplay*, September 1928.

"The Thistle and the Rose." *Exhibitor's Herald,* November 26, 1921.

"The Winners Are Announced." *Motion Picture Classic*, December 1920.

"Theater Manager Faces Check Charge." *Oakland Tribune* (CA), November 28, 1935.

"This Is Not Mrs. Vernon Castle But a Davenport Girl for Whom Movie Critics Predict a Future." *Quad-City Times* (Davenport, IA), June 8, 1919.

"Threaten Mann Act Charge for Gene Brewster." *Atlanta Constitution* (GA), December 5, 1922.

"Titian Locks Won Her Place On Screen." *The Times Recorder* (Zanesville, OH), September 11, 1932.

"To Sell Effects of Corliss Palmer." *New York Times,* November 17, 1926.

"Tom Terriss Gives Us a Few Refreshing Departures." *The Film Spectator*, June 23, 1928.

"Tropical Love Drama Will Open Today." *Los Angeles Times,* April 10, 1927.

"Tropical Play Gives Way to One Near Home." *Los Angeles Times*, April 22, 1927.

"Two Girls from South Win Fame and Beauty Contest." *Exhibitors Herald*, December 4, 1920.

"Two Wives, Affinity and Love Glossary." *The Coosa River News* (AL), January 5, 1923.

"Veidt's Future is Assured By 'A Man's Past.'" *The Palm Beach Post* (FL), December 4, 1927.

"Waiting." *Brooklyn Daily Eagle* (NY), April 20, 1932.

"We Announce the American Beauty." *Motion Picture*, July 1923.

"Wedding of Millions 5 Years Ago! Remarriage Finds Love Alone Left." *The Star Press* (Muncie, IN), March 21, 1931.

"Who's Who in the Film Game." *Motography*, Christmas 1913.

"Wife Accuses Executive in Divorce Suit." *Detroit Free Press*, June 27, 1947.

"Wife and Millions Lost, Brewster edits Mss. At 40¢ Per 1,000." *Variety*, November 10, 1931.

"Wife No. 1 is After Brewster." *The Southeast Missourian*, November 24, 1926.

"Wife Sues Brewster Over Girl Protégé." *New York Herald*, December 2, 1922.

"William Lord Wright's Page." *The Moving Picture News*, May 18, 1912.

"William Russell Hervey." *FindAGrave*. Web. Accessed April 12, 2017. (https://www.findagrave.com/cgi-bin/fg.cgi?page=gr&GRid= 12309991)

"Winners May Star in Fan Magazine Picture." *Exhibitors Herald*, December 11, 1920.

"Woes of Lovesick Brewster and his Millions—1924 Edition." *The Vancouver Daily World* (British Columbia, Canada), March 1, 1924.

Ad for Brewster auction, *Los Angeles Times*, November 27, 1927.

Advertisement featuring Al Cohen clients, *Film Daily Year Book*, 1931.

Advertisement for "100 Helps to Live 100 Years." *Brooklyn Daily Eagle* (NY), September 22, 1935.

Advertisement for "A Dream of Fair Women." *Shadowland*, November 1919.

Advertisement for Brewster-Palmer auction, *Brooklyn Daily Eagle* (NY), April 3, 1924.

Advertisement for Liane Hill as literary assistant, *Brooklyn Daily Eagle*, October 1, 1935.

Advertisement for the "American Beauty Contest," *Motion Picture*, June 1922.

Advertisement for the work of S.S. Millard, *Film Daily Year Book*, 1929.

Advertisement for Ventura County Church of Religious Science, *Press-Courier* (Oxnard, CA), July 4, 1976.

Advertisement introducing *Beauty* Magazine, *Motion Picture Classic*, May 1922.

Albert J. Cohen / Estelle R. Albus, Ancestry.com. Philadelphia, Pennsylvania, Marriage Index, 1885-1951 [database on-line]. Provo, UT, USA: Ancestry.com Operations, Inc., 2011.Original data: "Pennsylvania, Philadelphia Marriage Index, 1885–1951." Index. FamilySearch, Salt Lake City, Utah, 2009. Philadelphia County Pennsylvania Clerk of the Orphans' Court. "Pennsylvania, Philadelphia marriage license index, 1885-1951." Clerk of the Orphans' Court, Philadelphia, Pennsylvania.

Albert J. Cohen / Jeanne Sorel, California Department of Public Health, courtesy of www.vitalsearch-worldwide.com. Digital Images. Ancestry.com. California, County Birth, Marriage, and Death Records, 1849-1980 [database on-line]. Lehi, UT, USA: Ancestry.com Operations, Inc., 2017.Original data: California, County Birth, Marriage, and Death Records, 1830-1980. California Department of Public Health, courtesy of www.vitalsearch-worldwide.com. Digital Images.

Albert J. Cohen, Year: 1940; Census Place: Los Angeles, Los Angeles, California; Roll: T627_377; Page: 3B; Enumeration District: 60-1310. Ancestry.com. 1940 United States Federal Census [database on-line]. Provo, UT, USA: Ancestry.com Operations, Inc., 2012. Original data: United States of America, Bureau of the Census. Sixteenth Census of the United States, 1940. Washington, D.C.: National Archives and Records Administration, 1940. T627, 4,643 rolls.

Anderson, Nancy B. "Macon." *New Georgia Encyclopedia*, August 30, 2017. Web. Accessed August 31, 2017. (http://www.georgiaencyclopedia.org/articles/counties-cities-neighborhoods/macon)

Ankerich, Michael G. (2011). *Dangerous Curves Atop Hollywood Heels: The Lives, Careers, and Misfortunes of 14 Lard-Luck Girls of the Silent Screen*. BearManor Media.

Arthur Hopkins Papers, *T-Mss 1992-017. Billy Rose Theatre Division, The New York Public Library for the Performing Arts.

Ashbaugh, Don. "Broadway Fever: Not Too Contagious." *Motion Picture News*, March 16, 1929.

Barbato, Joan K. "Eleven Oaks has rich history of interesting owners." *The Daily Record* (Morristown, NJ), April 23, 1992.

Barbato, Joan. "Era passes at Weldon estate sale." *The Daily Record* (Morristown, NJ), June 22, 1984.

Belfrage, Cedric. "Clara Bow Exposed!" *Motion Picture Classic*, December 1928.

Bezecny, Adam. "The Mad Legacy: An Interview with Nick Millard." *The Liberal Dead*, July 17, 2012. Web. Accessed January 10, 2017. (http://liberaldead.com/blog/the-mad-legacy-an-interview-with-nick-millard/)

Blurb about "Red Kisses." *Pittsburg Post-Gazette* (PA), March 15, 1925.

Blurb about "Scarlet Youth," *Motion Picture News*, March 31, 1928.

Blurb about Al Cohen and family, *The Desert Sentinel* (Desert Hot Spring, CA), June 22, 1950.

Blurb about Brewster and "X-It," *The Princeton Alumni Weekly*, December 7, 1934.

Blurb about Corliss Palmer Productions, *The Editor*, April 18, 1921.

Blurb about Eugene and Liane Brewster's new address, *Brooklyn Daily Eagle* (NY), June 25, 1935.

Blurb about Jeanne Sorel, *Cine-Mundial*, September 1932.

Blurb about Julia and Luther Palmer's estate, *Quitman Advertiser* (GA), July 8, 1910.

Boney, F. N.. "Poor Whites." *New Georgia Encyclopedia*, May 16, 2016. Web. Accessed August 31, 2017. (http://www.georgiaencyclopedia.org/articles/history-archaeology/poor-whites)

Brennan, Lillian W. "A Review of Reviews." *Film Daily*, January 9, 1928.

Brewster, Eugene V. "Criticising [sic] Critics." *Motion Picture*, August 1926.

Brewster, Eugene V. "Hollywood Notes." *Motion Picture*, August 1, 1926.

Brewster, Eugene V. "Impressions of Hollywood." *Motion Picture*, May 1926.

Camarillo State Hospital Collection, Cal. State Univ., Channel Islands; Hospital History, 1/30; overview of hospital and procedures, circa 1957.

Camarillo State Hospital Collection, Cal. State Univ., Channel Islands; Hospital Programs, 2/2; Camarillo State Hospital brochure, October 1971.

Carless [sic] Brewster, Year: 1930; Census Place: Los Angeles, Los Angeles, California; Roll: 134; Page: 5A; Enumeration District: 0054; FHL microfilm: 2339869. Ancestry.com. 1930 United States Federal Census [database online]. Provo, UT, USA: Ancestry.com Operations Inc, 2002. Original data: United States of America, Bureau of the Census. Fifteenth Census of the United States, 1930. Washington, D.C.: National Archives and Records Administration, 1930. T626, 2,667 rolls.

Carliss [sic] Palmer, Year: 1920; Census Place: Macon Ward 4, Bibb, Georgia; Roll: T625_235; Page: 7B; Enumeration District: 43. Ancestry.com. 1920 United States Federal Census [database on-line]. Provo, UT, USA: Ancestry.com Operations, Inc., 2010. Images reproduced by FamilySearch. Original data: Fourteenth Census of the United States, 1920. (NARA microfilm publication T625, 2076 rolls). Records of the Bureau of the Census, Record Group 29. National Archives, Washington, D.C.

Caroline [sic] Palmer, Year: 1910; Census Place: Quitman, Brooks, Georgia; Roll: T624_174; Page: 12A; Enumeration District: 0017; FHL microfilm: 1374187. Ancestry.com. 1910 United States Federal Census [database online]. Provo, UT, USA: Ancestry.com Operations Inc, 2006. Original data:

Thirteenth Census of the United States, 1910 (NARA microfilm publication T624, 1,178 rolls). Records of the Bureau of the Census, Record Group 29. National Archives, Washington, D.C.

Certificate of Death: Corliss M. Taylor. Filed August 29, 1953, State of California, County of Ventura, Dept. of Health, Reg. Dist. No. 5690, State File No. 52-074955. Informant: Records of Camarillo State Hospital, Camarillo, CA.

Certificate of Death: Hoke Smith Palmer. Filed June 16, 1919. Commonwealth of Georgia, Bureau of Vital Statistics, State Board of Health. Reg. Dist. No. absent. State File No. 07071. Informant: Mrs. J.M. Simmone [mother of deceased], Macon, GA.

- Ch. 1: "Corliss Palmer Traces Rise in Life From Cabin in Georgia Cotton Field." October 22, 1933.
- Ch. 2: "Corliss Palmer Relates How She Went to New York On Inspiration By Picture." October 29, 1933.
- Ch. 3: "Ready to Flee Beauty Tests, Says Corliss." November 5, 1933.
- Ch. 4: "Patron's Love Surprised Her, Says Corliss." November 12, 1933.
- Ch. 5: "Corliss, Born in Cabin, Got Costly Estate." November 19, 1933.
- Ch. 6: "Corliss' Movie Career Ruined by Wife's Suit." November 26, 1933.
- Ch. 7: "Corliss Finds Fame, Sorrow in Hollywood." December 3, 1933.
- Ch. 8 (final): "Corliss Fights Off Suspicions of Gold Digging." December 10, 1933.

Cook, Joan. "Raymond J. Nagle, 90, Is Dead; Ex-Dean of Dentistry at N.Y.U." *New York Times*, June 20, 1991.

Corliss M. Taylor, Date: 1952-08-27. Ancestry.com. California, Death Index, 1940-1997 [database on-line]. Provo, UT, USA: Ancestry.com Operations Inc, 2000. Original data: State of California. California Death Index, 1940-1997. Sacramento, CA, USA: State of California Department of Health Services, Center for Health Statistics.

Cushing, Edward. "Music of the Day." *Brooklyn Daily Eagle* (NY), December 5, 1932.

Daly, Phil M. Jr. "Along the Rialto." *Film Daily*, February 12, 1930.

Denbo, Doris. "Beauty and the Rough Stuff." *Picture Play*, July 1925.

Dixon, Rob. "New South Era." *Encyclopedia of Alabama*, November 21, 2016. Web. Accessed September 14, 2017. (http://www.encyclopediaofalabama.org/article/h-2128)

Dumas, John. "Mrs. Brewster's Esperanto Party." *Imp of the Diverse*, April 18, 2015. Web. Accessed June 19, 2017. (http://impofthediverse.blogspot.com/2015/04/mrs-brewsters-esperanto-party.html)

Duncan A. Dobie Jr., Registration State: New York; Registration County: Queens; Roll: 1818486; Draft Board: 184. Ancestry.com. U.S., World War I Draft Registration Cards, 1917-1918 [database on-line]. Provo, UT, USA: Ancestry.com Operations Inc, 2005. Original data: United States, Selective Service System. World War I Selective Service System Draft Registration Cards, 1917-1918. Washington, D.C.: National Archives and Records Administration. M1509, 4,582 rolls. Imaged from Family History Library microfilm.

Duncan Albert Dobie, The National Archives at St. Louis; St. Louis, Missouri; Record Group Title: Records of the Selective Service System, 1926-1975; Record Group Number: 147. Ancestry.com. U.S., World War II Draft Registration Cards, 1942 [database on-line]. Lehi, UT, USA: Ancestry.com Operations, Inc., 2010. Original data: United States, Selective Service System. Selective Service Registration Cards, World War II: Fourth Registration. Records of the Selective Service System, Record Group Number 147. National Archives and Records Administration.

Duncan Dobie Jr., Year: 1930; Census Place: Islip, Suffolk, New York; Roll: 1650; Page: 30B; Enumeration District: 0082; FHL microfilm: 2341384. Ancestry.com. 1930 United States Federal Census [database on-line]. Provo, UT, USA: Ancestry.com Operations Inc, 2002. Original data: United States of America, Bureau of the Census. Fifteenth Census of the United States, 1930. Washington, D.C.: National Archives and Records Administration, 1930. T626, 2,667 rolls.

Dunn, Geoffrey. "The American Venus: Fay Lanphier's controversial career as Miss America." *Santa Cruz Public Library Local History*. Web. Accessed May 3, 2017. (https://history.santacruzpl.org/omeka/items/show/10859)

Emmis [sic] Palmer, Year: 1920; Census Place: Macon Ward 4, Bibb, Georgia; Roll: T625_235; Page: 7B; Enumeration District: 43. Ancestry.com. 1920 United States Federal Census [database on-line]. Provo, UT, USA: Ancestry.com Operations, Inc., 2010. Images reproduced by FamilySearch. Original data: Fourteenth Census of the United States, 1920. (NARA microfilm publication T625, 2076 rolls). Records of the Bureau of the Census, Record Group 29. National Archives, Washington, D.C.

Ennis Felton Purtell, Date: 1989-12-15. Ancestry.com. California, Death Index, 1940-1997 [database on-line]. Provo, UT, USA: Ancestry.com Operations Inc, 2000. Original data: State of California. California Death Index, 1940-1997. Sacramento, CA, USA: State of California Department of Health Services, Center for Health Statistics.

Eug V (Corliss) Brewster, 1930 Los Angeles City Directory, *LAPL Historic City and Business Directories*. Web. Accessed August 19, 2017. (http://rescarta.lapl.org:8080/ResCarta-Web/jsp/RcWebBrowse.jsp)

Eugene Brewster / Emilie Chinluck [sic], Ancestry.com. New York, New York, Marriage Certificate Index 1866-1937 [database on-line]. Provo, UT, USA: Ancestry.com Operations, Inc., 2014. Original data: Index to New York City Marriages, 1866-1937. Indices prepared by the Italian Genealogical Group and the German Genealogy Group, and used with permission of the New York City Department of Records/Municipal Archives.

Eugene Brewster, Year: 1870; Census Place: Islip, Suffolk, New York; Roll: M593_1101; Page: 35B; Family History Library Film: 552600. Ancestry.com. 1870 United States Federal Census [database on-line]. Provo, UT, USA: Ancestry. com Operations, Inc., 2009. Images reproduced by FamilySearch. Original data: 1870 U.S. census, population schedules. NARA microfilm publication M593, 1,761 rolls. Washington, D.C.: National Archives and Records Administration, n.d.

Eugene Brewster, Year: 1920; Census Place: North Hempstead, Nassau, New York; Roll: T625_1128; Page: 22A; Enumeration District: 61. Ancestry.com. 1920 United States Federal Census [database on-line]. Provo, UT, USA: Ancestry.com Operations, Inc., 2010. Images reproduced by FamilySearch. Original data: Fourteenth Census of the United States, 1920. (NARA microfilm publication T625, 2076 rolls). Records of the Bureau of the Census, Record Group 29. National Archives, Washington, D.C.

Eugene Brewster, Year: 1930; Census Place: Los Angeles, Los Angeles, California; Roll: 134; Page: 5A; Enumeration District: 0054; FHL microfilm: 2339869. Ancestry.com. 1930 United States Federal Census [database on-line]. Provo, UT, USA: Ancestry.com Operations Inc, 2002. Original data: United States of America, Bureau of the Census. Fifteenth Census of the United States, 1930. Washington, D.C.: National Archives and Records Administration, 1930. T626, 2,667 rolls.

Eugene V. Brewster, Year: 1910; Census Place: Brooklyn Ward 7, Kings, New York; Roll: T624_957; Page: 11B; Enumeration District: 0109; FHL microfilm: 1374970. Ancestry.com. 1910 United States Federal Census [database on-line]. Provo, UT, USA: Ancestry.com Operations Inc, 2006. Original data: Thirteenth Census of the United States, 1910 (NARA microfilm publication T624, 1,178 rolls). Records of the Bureau of the Census, Record Group 29. National Archives, Washington, D.C.

Fehr, Louis H. "Rolled Socks Won Brewster, Wife Declares." *The Washington Herald* (DC), December 6, 1922.

Fellers, Lou Ann. "Normandy Parkway converted carriage house has lush garden." *The Daily Record* (Morristown, NJ), June 19, 2016.

Florine D. Mercereau, Ancestry.com. Florida Death Index, 1877-1998 [database on-line]. Provo, UT, USA: Ancestry.com Operations Inc, 2004. Original data: State of Florida. Florida Death Index, 1877-1998. Florida: Florida Department of Health, Office of Vital Records, 1998.

Florine D. Mercereau, Ancestry.com. Florida, Divorce Index, 1927-2001 [database on-line]. Provo, UT, USA: Ancestry.com Operations Inc, 2005. Original data: Florida Department of Health. Florida Divorce Index, 1927-2001. Jacksonville, FL, USA: Florida Department of Health.

Florine Dehart Cain, Ancestry.com. Virginia, Divorce Records, 1918-2014 [database on-line]. Provo, UT, USA: Ancestry.com Operations, Inc., 2015. Original data: Virginia Divorce Records, 1918–2014. Virginia Department of Health, Richmond, Virginia.

Florine F. Dehart, Year: 1920; Census Place: Bristol Ward 2, Bristol (Independent City), Virginia; Roll: T625_1882; Page: 1B; Enumeration District: 10. Ancestry.com. 1920 United States Federal Census [database on-line]. Provo, UT, USA: Ancestry.com Operations, Inc., 2010. Images reproduced by FamilySearch. Original data: Fourteenth Census of the United States, 1920. (NARA microfilm publication T625, 2076 rolls). Records of the Bureau of the Census, Record Group 29. National Archives, Washington, D.C.

Florine Findlay De Hart, Ancestry.com. Virginia, Birth Records, 1912-2014, Delayed Birth Records, 1854-1911 [database on-line]. Provo, UT, USA: Ancestry.com Operations, Inc., 2015. Original data: Virginia, Births, 1864–2014. Virginia Department of Health, Richmond, Virginia.

Florrine [sic] Dehart Kane, Year: 1930; Census Place: Bristol, Bristol (Independent City), Virginia; Roll: 2466; Page: 4B; Enumeration District: 0004; FHL microfilm: 2342200. Ancestry.com. 1930 United States Federal Census [database on-line]. Provo, UT, USA: Ancestry.com Operations Inc, 2002. Original data: United States of America, Bureau of the Census. Fifteenth Census of the United States, 1930. Washington, D.C.: National Archives and Records Administration, 1930. T626, 2,667 rolls.

Fowler, Gene. "E.V. Brewster Tells His Own Tale of Love." *The Bee* (Dansville, VA), December 6, 1922.

Fowler, Gene. "His Children Approve Love, Says Brewster." *The Washington Herald* (DC), December 6. 1922.

Fowler, Gene. "Rich Wife Too Vain to Keep Love of Him, Says Brewster, Who Now Likes Miss Palmer." *San Antonio Evening News* (TX), December 5, 1922.

Frankel, Aaron. "Potassium permanganate: The Most Useful Survival Chemical." *In the Rabbit Hole*, July 28th, 2011. Web. Accessed June 26, 2017. (https://www.intherabbithole.com/potassium-permanganate-the-most-useful-survival-chemical/)

Frost, Mary. "5 A.M. demolition at former Long Island College Hospital (LICH) riles Brooklyn neighbors." *Brooklyn Daily Eagle* website, February 3, 2017. Web. Accessed February 16, 2017. (http://www.brooklyneagle.com/articles/2017/2/3/5-am-demolition-former-long-island-college-hospital-lich-riles-brooklyn-neighbors)

Garza, Janiss. "Synopsis: Bromo and Juliet (1926)." *AllMovie*. Web. Accessed February 8, 2016. (https://www.allmovie.com/movie/bromo-and-juliet-v228673)

Geo. J. Purtell, Year: 1920; Census Place: Morristown Ward 2, Morris, New Jersey; Roll: T625_1060; Page: 5A; Enumeration District: 34. Ancestry.com. 1920 United States Federal Census [database on-line]. Provo, UT, USA: Ancestry.com Operations, Inc., 2010. Images reproduced by FamilySearch. Original data: Fourteenth Census of the United States, 1920. (NARA microfilm publication T625, 2076 rolls). Records of the Bureau of the Census, Record Group 29. National Archives, Washington, D.C.

George J Portell [sic], Year: 1940; Census Place: Santa Monica, Los Angeles, California; Roll: T627_257; Page: 12A; Enumeration District: 19-773. Ancestry.com. 1940 United States Federal Census [database on-line]. Provo, UT, USA: Ancestry. com Operations, Inc., 2012. Original data: United States of America, Bureau of the Census. Sixteenth Census of the United States, 1940. Washington, D.C.: National Archives and Records Administration, 1940. T627, 4,643 rolls.

Gevinson, Alan, and AFI (1997). *Within Our Gates: Ethnicity In American Feature Films, 1911-1960 (The American Film Institute Catalog of Motion Pictures Produced in the United States).* 1st ed. University of California Press.

Gifford, Denis. "James Stuart Blackton." *Who's Who of Victorian Cinema.* Web. Accessed February 12, 2016. http://www.victorian-cinema.net/blackton

Gordon, Samuel M., and Eleanore B. Dufour. "Pyorrhea Quackery." *Hygeia,* May 1937.

Grady M. [sic] Palmer, Ancestry.com. U.S., Headstone Applications for Military Veterans, 1925-1963 [database on-line]. Provo, UT, USA: Ancestry.com Operations, Inc., 2012. Original data: Applications for Headstones for U.S. Military Veterans, 1925-1941. Microfilm publication M1916, 134 rolls. ARC ID: 596118. Records of the Office of the Quartermaster General, Record Group 92. National Archives at Washington, D.C.

Grady Palmer, Ancestry.com. U.S. City Directories, 1822-1995 [database on-line]. Provo, UT, USA: Ancestry.com Operations, Inc., 2011. Original data: Glendale, California, City Directory, 1939.

Grady Palmer, Ancestry.com. U.S. City Directories, 1822-1995 [database on-line]. Provo, UT, USA: Ancestry.com Operations, Inc., 2011. Original data: Morristown, New Jersey, City Directory, 1933.

Grady Palmer, Year: 1920; Census Place: Macon Ward 4, Bibb, Georgia; Roll: T625_235; Page: 7B; Enumeration District: 43. Ancestry.com. 1920 United States Federal Census [database on-line]. Provo, UT, USA: Ancestry.com Operations, Inc., 2010. Images reproduced by FamilySearch. Original data: Fourteenth Census of the United States, 1920. (NARA microfilm publication T625, 2076 rolls). Records of the Bureau of the Census, Record Group 29. National Archives, Washington, D.C.

Grady Palmer, Year: 1940; Census Place: Glendale, Los Angeles, California; Roll: T627_231; Page: 4A; Enumeration District: 19-219. Ancestry.com. 1940

United States Federal Census [database on-line]. Provo, UT, USA: Ancestry. com Operations, Inc., 2012. Original data: United States of America, Bureau of the Census. Sixteenth Census of the United States, 1940. Washington, D.C.: National Archives and Records Administration, 1940. T627, 4,643 rolls.

Grady Watterson Palmer, Date: 1950-03-05. Ancestry.com. California, Death Index, 1940-1997 [database on-line]. Provo, UT, USA: Ancestry.com Operations Inc, 2000. Original data: State of California. California Death Index, 1940-1997. Sacramento, CA, USA: State of California Department of Health Services, Center for Health Statistics.

Gray, Mollie. "Gray Matter: Miss Palmer Again." *Variety,* May 22, 1929.

Hall, Gladys. "A Star in the Dawning." *Motion Picture*, March 1921.

Hall, Mordaunt. "The Screen." Review of "A Man's Past," October 4, 1927.

Hall, Mordaunt. "The Screen." Review of "The Night Bird." *New York Times,* October 2, 1928.

Harris, Ruth Mary. "A Lesson in Vamping." *Picture-Play*, July 1923.

Haynes, Ruth Tremont. "The Tell-Tale Mouth." *Beauty*, February 1922.

Hazel Keener / Ross Chatelain, Ancestry.com. Michigan, Marriage Records, 1867-1952 [database on-line]. Provo, UT, USA: Ancestry.com Operations, Inc., 2015. Original data: Michigan, Marriage Records, 1867–1952. Michigan Department of Community Health, Division for Vital Records and Health Statistics.

Hoke S. Palmer, Ancestry.com. Georgia, World War I Service Cards, 1917-1919 [database on-line]. Provo, UT, USA: Ancestry.com Operations, Inc., 2013. Original data: Georgia Adjutant General's Office. World War I Statements of Service Cards. Georgia State Archives, Morrow, Georgia.

Hoke Smith Palmer, Ancestry.com. Georgia, Deaths Index, 1914-1927 [database on-line]. Provo, UT, USA: Ancestry.com Operations, Inc., 2011. Original data: "Georgia Deaths, 1914–1927." Index. FamilySearch, Salt Lake City, Utah, 2007. "Georgia Deaths, 1914–1927" and "Georgia Deaths, 1930," images, Family-Search. Georgia Department of Health and Vital Statistics, Atlanta, Georgia.

J.M. Simmone, Year: 1920; Census Place: Macon Ward 4, Bibb, Georgia; Roll: T625_235; Page: 7B; Enumeration District: 43. Ancestry.com. 1920 United States Federal Census [database on-line]. Provo, UT, USA: Ancestry.com Operations, Inc., 2010. Images reproduced by FamilySearch. Original data: Fourteenth Census of the United States, 1920. (NARA microfilm publication T625, 2076 rolls). Records of the Bureau of the Census, Record Group 29. National Archives, Washington, D.C.

Jack Dehart Kane, Ancestry.com. Virginia, Birth Records, 1912-2014, Delayed Birth Records, 1854-1911 [database on-line]. Provo, UT, USA: Ancestry.com Operations, Inc., 2015. Original data: Virginia, Births, 1864–2014. Virginia Department of Health, Richmond, Virginia.

James C. Palmer / Jean L. Smith, Ancestry.com. California, Marriage Index, 1949-1959 [database on-line]. Provo, UT, USA: Ancestry.com Operations, Inc., 2013. Original data: California Department of Health and Welfare. California Vital Records—Vitalsearch (www.vitalsearch-worldwide.com). The Vitalsearch Company Worldwide, Inc., Pleasanton, California.

James Calvin Palmer, Ancestry.com. U.S., Headstone Applications for Military Veterans, 1925-1963 [database on-line]. Provo, UT, USA: Ancestry.com Operations, Inc., 2012. Original data: Applications for Headstones for U.S. Military Veterans, 1925-1941. Microfilm publication M1916, 134 rolls. ARC ID: 596118. Records of the Office of the Quartermaster General, Record Group 92. National Archives at Washington, D.C.

James Palmer, Year: 1930; Census Place: Los Angeles, Los Angeles, California; Roll: 134; Page: 5A; Enumeration District: 0054; FHL microfilm: 2339869. Ancestry.com. 1930 United States Federal Census [database on-line]. Provo, UT, USA: Ancestry.com Operations Inc, 2002. Original data: United States of America, Bureau of the Census. Fifteenth Census of the United States, 1930. Washington, D.C.: National Archives and Records Administration, 1930. T626, 2,667 rolls.

James Simmone (Julia), Ancestry.com. U.S. City Directories, 1822-1995 [database on-line]. Provo, UT, USA: Ancestry.com Operations, Inc., 2011. Original data: Macon, Georgia, City Directory, 1915.

Janice Preston, Year: 1940; Census Place: Atlanta, Fulton, Georgia; Roll: T627_725; Page: 1B; Enumeration District: 160-27. Ancestry.com. 1940 United States Federal Census [database on-line]. Provo, UT, USA: Ancestry.com Operations, Inc., 2012. Original data: United States of America, Bureau of the Census. Sixteenth Census of the United States, 1940. Washington, D.C.: National Archives and Records Administration, 1940. T627, 4,643 rolls.

Jno [sic] T. Dehart, Year: 1940; Census Place: Bristol, Bristol City, Virginia; Roll: T627_4305; Page: 8B; Enumeration District: 102-4. Ancestry.com. 1940 United States Federal Census [database on-line]. Provo, UT, USA: Ancestry.com Operations, Inc., 2012. Original data: United States of America, Bureau of the Census. Sixteenth Census of the United States, 1940. Washington, D.C.: National Archives and Records Administration, 1940. T627, 4,643 rolls.

John R. Ferrell / Eldora Patterson, Ancestry.com. Alabama, County Marriages, 1805-1967 [database on-line]. Lehi, UT, USA: Ancestry.com Operations, Inc., 2016. Original data: Marriage Records. Alabama Marriages. FamilySearch, Salt Lake City, UT.

John R. Ferrell, Year: 1880; Census Place: Providence, Chilton, Alabama; Roll: 6; Family History Film: 1254006; Page: 17D; Enumeration District: 027. Ancestry.com and The Church of Jesus Christ of Latter-day Saints. 1880 United States Federal Census [database on-line]. Lehi, UT, USA: Ancestry.com Operations Inc, 2010. 1880 U.S. Census Index provided by The Church of Jesus Christ of Latter-day Saints © Copyright 1999 Intellectual Reserve, Inc. All rights reserved. Original data: Tenth Census of the United States, 1880. (NARA microfilm publication T9, 1,454 rolls). Records of the Bureau of the Census, Record Group 29. National Archives, Washington, D.C.

Julia A. Simmone, Ancestry.com. U.S. City Directories, 1822-1995 [database on-line]. Provo, UT, USA: Ancestry.com Operations, Inc., 2011. Original data: Macon, Georgia, City Directory, 1922.

Julia Alma Simmone, Year: 1920; Census Place: Macon Ward 4, Bibb, Georgia; Roll: T625_235; Page: 7B; Enumeration District: 43. Ancestry.com. 1920 United States Federal Census [database on-line]. Provo, UT, USA: Ancestry.com Operations, Inc., 2010. Images reproduced by FamilySearch. Original data: Fourteenth Census of the United States, 1920. (NARA microfilm publication T625, 2076 rolls). Records of the Bureau of the Census, Record Group 29. National Archives, Washington, D.C

Julia Fer [sic] Palmer, Ancestry.com. U.S., Social Security Applications and Claims Index, 1936-2007 [database on-line]. Provo, UT, USA: Ancestry.com Operations, Inc., 2015. Original data: Social Security Applications and Claims, 1936-2007.

Julia Ferrell, Year: 1880; Census Place: Providence, Chilton, Alabama; Roll: 6; Family History Film: 1254006; Page: 17D; Enumeration District: 027. Ancestry.com and The Church of Jesus Christ of Latter-day Saints. 1880 United States Federal Census [database on-line]. Lehi, UT, USA: Ancestry.com Operations Inc, 2010. 1880 U.S. Census Index provided by The Church of Jesus Christ of Latter-day Saints © Copyright 1999 Intellectual Reserve, Inc. All rights reserved. Original data: Tenth Census of the United States, 1880. (NARA microfilm publication T9, 1,454 rolls). Records of the Bureau of the Census, Record Group 29. National Archives, Washington, D.C.

Julia Palmer Jr., Year: 1930; Census Place: Los Angeles, Los Angeles, California; Roll: 134; Page: 5A; Enumeration District: 0054; FHL microfilm: 2339869. Ancestry.com. 1930 United States Federal Census [database on-line]. Provo, UT, USA: Ancestry.com Operations Inc, 2002. Original data: United States of America, Bureau of the Census. Fifteenth Census of the United States, 1930. Washington, D.C.: National Archives and Records Administration, 1930. T626, 2,667 rolls.

Julia Palmer, 1932 Los Angeles City Directory, *LAPL Historic City and Business Directories*. Web. Accessed August 19, 2017. (http://rescarta.lapl.org:8080/ResCarta-Web/jsp/RcWebBrowse.jsp)

Julia Palmer, 1934 Los Angeles City Directory, *LAPL Historic City and Business Directories*. Web. Accessed August 19, 2017. (http://rescarta.lapl.org:8080/ResCarta-Web/jsp/RcWebBrowse.jsp)

Julia Palmer, Year: 1940; Census Place: Glendale, Los Angeles, California; Roll: T627_231; Page: 4A; Enumeration District: 19-219. Ancestry.com. 1940 United States Federal Census [database on-line]. Provo, UT, USA: Ancestry.com Operations, Inc., 2012. Original data: United States of America, Bureau of the Census. Sixteenth Census of the United States, 1940. Washington, D.C.: National Archives and Records Administration, 1940. T627, 4,643 rolls.

Jungmeyer, Jack. "Hollywood! by Russell J. Birdwell." *Santa Ana Register* (CA), May 4, 1926.

Katherine Frederickson, Year: 1940; Census Place: Glendale, Los Angeles, California; Roll: T627_229; Page: 13A; Enumeration District: 19-176. Ancestry. com. 1940 United States Federal Census [database on-line]. Provo, UT, USA: Ancestry.com Operations, Inc., 2012. Original data: United States of America, Bureau of the Census. Sixteenth Census of the United States, 1940. Washington, D.C.: National Archives and Records Administration, 1940. T627, 4,643 rolls.

Krug, Karl B. "Harris—Vaudeville and Photoplays." *The Pittsburg Press* (PA), September 18, 1928.

Lane, Tamar. "Much Ado About Nothing." *The Film Mercury,* June 11, 1926.

Lee, Dan P. "Peaches: Who's Your Daddy?" *New York Magazine,* April 9, 2012.

Liane Brewster, Year: 1935; Arrival: New York, New York; Microfilm Serial: T715, 1897-1957; Microfilm Roll: Roll 5691; Line: 27; Page Number: 117. Ancestry.com. New York, Passenger Lists, 1820-1957 [database on-line]. Provo, UT, USA: Ancestry.com Operations, Inc., 2010. Original data: Passenger Lists of Vessels Arriving at New York, New York, 1820-1897. Microfilm Publication M237, 675 rolls. NAI: 6256867. Records of the U.S. Customs Service, Record Group 36. National Archives at Washington, D.C.

Liane Brewster, Year: 1940; Census Place: New York, Kings, New York; Roll: T627_2547; Page: 82A; Enumeration District: 24-30. Ancestry.com. 1940 United States Federal Census [database on-line]. Provo, UT, USA: Ancestry.com Operations, Inc., 2012. Original data: United States of America, Bureau of the Census. Sixteenth Census of the United States, 1940. Washington, D.C.: National Archives and Records Administration, 1940. T627, 4,643 rolls.

Lindquist, Christine (August 1, 2017). Phone interview with author.

List of wounded, degree undetermined. *Washington Post,* August 11, 1918.

Lowe, Denise (2004). *An Encyclopedic Dictionary of Women in Early American Films: 1895-1930.* 1st ed. Routledge.

Luther M. Palmer, Year: 1910; Census Place: Quitman, Brooks, Georgia; Roll: T624_174; Page: 12A; Enumeration District: 0017; FHL microfilm: 1374187. Ancestry.com. 1910 United States Federal Census [database on-line]. Provo, UT, USA: Ancestry.com Operations Inc, 2006. Original data: Thirteenth Census of the United States, 1910 (NARA microfilm publication T624, 1,178 rolls). Records of the Bureau of the Census, Record Group 29. National Archives, Washington, D.C.

Maria T. Brewster, Ancestry.com. New York, New York, Marriage Certificate Index 1866-1937 [database on-line]. Provo, UT, USA: Ancestry.com Operations, Inc., 2014. Original data: Index to New York City Marriages, 1866-1937. Indices prepared by the Italian Genealogical Group and the German Genealogy Group, and used with permission of the New York City Department of Records/Municipal Archives.

Marie T Brewster, New York City Municipal Archives; New York, New York; Borough: Brooklyn. Ancestry.com. New York City, Marriage License Indexes, 1907-1995 [database on-line]. Lehi, UT, USA: Ancestry.com Operations, Inc., 2017. Original data: New York City Clerk's Office, New York, New York.

Mary E Preston, Ancestry.com. U.S. City Directories, 1822-1995 [database on-line]. Provo, UT, USA: Ancestry.com Operations, Inc., 2011. Original data: Newark, New Jersey, City Directory, 1938.

Mary E Preston, Date: 1969-06-04. Ancestry.com. California, Death Index, 1940-1997 [database on-line]. Provo, UT, USA: Ancestry.com Operations Inc, 2000. Original data: State of California. California Death Index, 1940-1997. Sacramento, CA, USA: State of California Department of Health Services, Center for Health Statistics.

Mary Emma Palmer / Oscar David Preston, Ancestry.com. Georgia, Marriage Records From Select Counties, 1828-1978 [database on-line]. Provo, UT, USA: Ancestry.com Operations, Inc., 2013. Original data: County Marriage Records, 1828–1978. The Georgia Archives, Morrow, Georgia.

Mildred Bowling, Year: 1910; Census Place: Baltimore Ward 6, Baltimore (Independent City), Maryland; Roll: T624_554; Page: 18A; Enumeration District: 0060; FHL microfilm: 1374567. Ancestry.com. 1910 United States Federal Census [database on-line]. Provo, UT, USA: Ancestry.com Operations Inc, 2006. Original data: Thirteenth Census of the United States, 1910 (NARA microfilm publication T624, 1,178 rolls). Records of the Bureau of the Census, Record Group 29. National Archives, Washington, D.C

Mildred Bowling, Year: 1920; Census Place: Baltimore Ward 6, Baltimore (Independent City), Maryland; Roll: T625_660; Page: 15A; Enumeration District: 70. Ancestry.com. 1920 United States Federal Census [database on-line]. Provo, UT, USA: Ancestry.com Operations, Inc., 2010. Images reproduced by FamilySearch. Original data: Fourteenth Census of the United States, 1920. (NARA microfilm publication T625, 2076 rolls). Records of the Bureau of the Census, Record Group 29. National Archives, Washington, D.C.

National Register of Historic Places, Normandy Park Historic District, Morris Township, Morris County, New Jersey, National Register #96001469.

Oscar D Preston, Georgia Health Department, Office of Vital Records; Georgia, USA; Indexes of Vital Records for Georgia: Deaths, 1919-1998; Certificate Number: 5789. Ancestry.com. Georgia, Death Index, 1919-1998 [database on-line]. Provo, UT, USA: Ancestry.com Operations Inc, 2001. Original data: State of Georgia. Indexes of Vital Records for Georgia: Deaths, 1919-1998. Georgia, USA: Georgia Health Department, Office of Vital Records, 1998.

Oscar Palmer [sic], Year: 1930; Census Place: Morristown, Morris, New Jersey; Roll: 1374; Page: 6B; Enumeration District: 0045; FHL microfilm: 2341109. Ancestry.com. 1930 United States Federal Census [database on-line]. Provo, UT, USA: Ancestry.com Operations Inc, 2002. Original data: United States of America, Bureau of the Census. Fifteenth Census of the United States, 1930. Washington, D.C.: National Archives and Records Administration, 1930. T626, 2,667 rolls.

Palmer Purtell [sic], Year: 1930; Census Place: Los Angeles, Los Angeles, California; Roll: 135; Page: 14A; Enumeration District: 0079; FHL microfilm: 2339870. Ancestry.com. 1930 United States Federal Census [database on-line]. Provo, UT, USA: Ancestry.com Operations Inc, 2002. Original data: United States of America, Bureau of the Census. Fifteenth Census of the United States, 1930. Washington, D.C.: National Archives and Records Administration, 1930. T626, 2,667 rolls.

Palmer, Corliss. "A Movie Star Confesses—I Ruined My Hollywood Career. *True Confessions*, June 1942.

Palmer, Corliss. "As Pearls of the Orient." *Motion Picture*, September 1921.

Palmer, Corliss. "Beauty's Crown." *Motion Picture*, May 1921.

Palmer, Corliss. "Boudoir Secrets of Famous Beauties." *Beauty*, February 1922.

Palmer, Corliss. "Every Woman's Fairy Godmother." *Motion Picture*, June 1921.

Palmer, Corliss. "In League With the Fairies." *Motion Picture*, April 1921.

Palmer, Corliss. "Restoration." *Motion Picture*, June 1922.

Palmer, Corliss. "Smiling Eyes." *Motion Picture,* May 1922.

Palmer, Corliss. "The Beauty Box." *Beauty*, February 1922.

Palmer, Corliss. "The Democracy of Beauty." *Motion Picture*, April 1922.

Palmer, Corliss. Serialized life story, *Milwaukee Sentinel* (WI):

Parsons, Louella. "Jeanne Sorel Film Colony's Latest 'Find.'" *Pittsburg Post-Gazette* (PA), March 28, 1932.

Patricia J. Merrill, Date: 1986-08-21. Ancestry.com. California, Death Index, 1940-1997 [database on-line]. Provo, UT, USA: Ancestry.com Operations Inc, 2000. Original data: State of California. California Death Index, 1940-1997.

Sacramento, CA, USA: State of California Department of Health Services, Center for Health Statistics.

Rafael Brewster, Year: 1930; Census Place: Islip, Suffolk, New York; Roll: 1650; Page: 18A; Enumeration District: 0082; FHL microfilm: 2341384. Ancestry.com. 1930 United States Federal Census [database on-line]. Provo, UT, USA: Ancestry.com Operations Inc, 2002. Original data: United States of America, Bureau of the Census. Fifteenth Census of the United States, 1930. Washington, D.C.: National Archives and Records Administration, 1930. T626, 2,667 rolls.

Rafael Brewster, Year: 1940; Census Place: Evanston, Cook, Illinois; Roll: T627_778; Page: 7A; Enumeration District: 16-185. Ancestry.com. 1940 United States Federal Census [database on-line]. Provo, UT, USA: Ancestry.com Operations, Inc., 2012. Original data: United States of America, Bureau of the Census. Sixteenth Census of the United States, 1940. Washington, D.C.: National Archives and Records Administration, 1940. T627, 4,643 rolls.

Randorf, William. "Brewster Rival is Jilted." *The Washington Times* (DC), December 7, 1922.

Redmond, Jennifer Ann (2016). *Reels & Rivals: Sisters in Silent Film.* BearManor Media.

S.D., Trav. "Peggy Hopkins Joyce: The Original Gold Digger." *Travalanche,* May 26, 2010. Web. Accessed October 20, 2016. (https://travsd.wordpress.com/2010/05/26/stars-of-vaudeville-160-peggy-hopkins-joyce/)

Sanders, Irwin T. and Douglas Ensminger (1940). "Alabama Rural Communities: A Study of Chilton County." *Alabama State College for Women Bulletin,* Vol. XXXIII, No. 1A.

Sarg. "Honeymoon Hate." *Moving Picture World,* December 17, 1927.

Schaefer, Eric (1999). *Bold! Daring! Shocking! True: A History of Exploitation Films, 1919-1959.* Duke University Press.

Sewell, C.S. "Reviews of Little Pictures with a Big Punch: 'Bromo and Juliet.'" *Moving Picture World,* September 25, 1926.

Shaffer, Rosalind. "Corliss Palmer, Georgia Peach, A Changed Girl." *Chicago Sunday Tribune,* June 10, 1934.

Shaffer, Rosalind. "Felix Knight Puts His Art Above Wealth." *Chicago Tribune,* February 10, 1935.

Shan. "Picture Brides." *Variety,* May 29, 1934.

Shelton, Louise (1916). *Beautiful Gardens in America.* 2nd ed. Charles Scribner's Sons.

Sherman, Beatrice. "Latest Works of Fiction: A Shattered Life." Review of *Year by Candlelight. New York Times,* April 14, 1941.

Shields, Dr. David S. "Samuel Lumiere." *Broadway Photographs*. Web. Accessed May 5, 2017. (http://broadway.cas.sc.edu/content/samuel-lumiere)

Shippey, Lee. "Lee Side o' L.A.: Personal Glimpses of World-Famed Southlanders." *Los Angeles Times,* July 7, 1929.

Sint S. Millard, Date: 1962-05-03. Ancestry.com. California, Death Index, 1940-1997 [database on-line]. Provo, UT, USA: Ancestry.com Operations Inc, 2000. Original data: State of California. California Death Index, 1940-1997. Sacramento, CA, USA: State of California Department of Health Services, Center for Health Statistics.

Slide, Anthony (2010). *Inside the Hollywood Fan Magazine: A History of Star Makers, Fabricators, and Gossip Mongers.* University Press of Mississippi.

Smith, Chester J. "A Man's Past: Tensely Dramatic and Well Done." *Motion Picture News*, September 16, 1927.

Stafford, M. Oakley. "Informing You." *Hartford Courant* (CT), December 16, 1955.

Stanton Palmer, Georgia Health Department, Office of Vital Records; Georgia, USA; Indexes of Vital Records for Georgia: Deaths, 1919-1998; Certificate Number: 20602. Ancestry.com. Georgia, Death Index, 1919-1998 [database on-line]. Provo, UT, USA: Ancestry.com Operations Inc, 2001.Original data: State of Georgia. Indexes of Vital Records for Georgia: Deaths, 1919-1998. Georgia, USA: Georgia Health Department, Office of Vital Records, 1998.

Stanton Palmer, Year: 1930; Census Place: Morristown, Morris, New Jersey; Roll: 1374; Page: 6B; Enumeration District: 0045; FHL microfilm: 2341109. Ancestry. com. 1930 United States Federal Census [database on-line]. Provo, UT, USA: Ancestry.com Operations Inc, 2002. Original data: United States of America, Bureau of the Census. Fifteenth Census of the United States, 1930. Washington, D.C.: National Archives and Records Administration, 1930. T626, 2,667 rolls.

Strausbaugh, John. "Brooklyn's Home to the Gentry and the Not-So." *New York Times* website, October 2, 2008. Web. Accessed February 16, 2017. (http://www.nytimes.com/2008/10/03/arts/03expl.html)

Stenn, David (1988). *Clara Bow: Runnin' Wild.* Doubleday.

Swinnerton, Ashley, MoMA Film Study Center. "Re: Status of 'The Noose.'" Message to author, June 29, 2017. E-mail.

The Church of Jesus Christ of Latter-day Saints, "Ancestral File," database, *FamilySearch* (https://familysearch.org/ark:/61903/2:1:MWLP-KDQ : accessed 02-02-2016), entry for Luther M. PALMER.

The Church of Jesus Christ of Latter-day Saints, "Ancestral File," database, *FamilySearch* (https://familysearch.org/ark:/61903/2:1:MWLP-2SS : accessed 01-20-2016), entry for Margaret Katherine GIANNINI.

*The Quin-decennial Record of the Class of '93 of Princeton University* (June 1908), Class of 1893, Princeton University.

Various advertisements from *Beauty*, February 1922.

W.R. Middleton / Anna Lyons, Ancestry.com. Florida, County Marriages, 1823-1982 [database on-line]. Lehi, UT, USA: Ancestry.com Operations, Inc., 2016. Original data: Marriage Records. Florida Marriages. FamilySearch, Salt Lake City, UT.

W.R. Middleton, Ancestry.com. Atlanta, Georgia, U.S. Penitentiary, Prisoner Index, ca. 1880-1922 [database on-line]. Provo, UT, USA: Ancestry.com Operations, Inc., 2009. Original data: Index to Atlanta Federal Penitentiary, Inmate Case Files, 1902-1921. [CD]. NARA Southeast Region (Atlanta) (NRCA), 5780 Jonesboro Road, Morrow, Georgia 30260.

Wahl, Jessica. "Miss Mary Nolan." *Silence is Platinum*, October 22, 2011. Web. Accessed August 8, 2017. (http://silenceisplatinum.blogspot.com/2011/10/miss-mary-nolan.html)

Wallace Woodward Mercereau / Florine Dehart Kane, Ancestry.com. Florida Marriage Indexes, 1822-1875 and 1927-2001 [database on-line]. Provo, UT, USA: Ancestry.com Operations Inc, 2006. Original data: Florida Department of Health. Florida Marriage Index, 1927-2001. Florida Department of Health, Jacksonville, Florida.

*Who's Who in New York City and State: a biographical dictionary of contemporaries.* W.F. Brainard, 1911.

Wilk, Ralph. "A Little from 'Lots.'" *Film Daily*, April 1, 1932.

Wilk, Ralph. "A Little from 'Lots.'" *Film Daily*, June 14, 1932.

William M. Taylor, Ancestry.com. U.S. City Directories, 1822-1995 [database on-line]. Provo, UT, USA: Ancestry.com Operations, Inc., 2011. Original data: Santa Monica, California, City Directory, 1947.

William M. Taylor, Ancestry.com. U.S. City Directories, 1822-1995 [database on-line]. Provo, UT, USA: Ancestry.com Operations, Inc., 2011. Original data: Glendale, California, City Directory, 1953.

William M. Taylor, Ancestry.com. U.S. City Directories, 1822-1995 [database on-line]. Provo, UT, USA: Ancestry.com Operations, Inc., 2011. Original data: Glendale, California, City Directory, 1951.

William M. Taylor, Year: 1940; Census Place: Los Angeles, Los Angeles, California; Roll: T627_393; Page: 14A; Enumeration District: 60-87. Ancestry.com. 1940 United States Federal Census [database on-line]. Provo, UT, USA: Ancestry.com Operations, Inc., 2012. Original data: United States of America, Bureau of the Census. Sixteenth Census of the United States, 1940. Washington, D.C.: National Archives and Records Administration, 1940. T627, 4,643 rolls.

*Woman's Who's Who of America, 1914-1915 ed.* Original publisher: New York: The American Commonwealth Company. Republished 1976, Gale Research Company, Book Tower, Detroit.

Woolridge, A.L. "Moral—Don't Win A Beauty Contest!" *Picture Play*, May 1927.

Xie, Julie. "Barbara Spiegelman, artist, homemaker." Obituary. *Philadelphia Inquirer*, April 26, 2014.

Yang, Zhongshu and Glen L. Xiong, *et.al.* (2015, Dec. 3). "Alcohol-Related Psychosis." *Medscape.* Retrieved March 21, 2017 from https://emedicine.medscape.com/article/289848-overview

Zaiman, Jack. "A Man, A Woman, A Stretch of Street." *Hartford Courant* (CT), September 12, 1949.

Zainaldin, Jamil S., and John C. Inscoe. "Progressive Era." *New Georgia Encyclopedia*, September 22, 2015. Web. Accessed August 31, 2017. (http://www.georgiaencyclopedia.org/articles/history-archaeology/progressive-era)

# INDEX

# ABOUT THE AUTHOR

Jennifer Ann Redmond found her calling at age seven, when her essay won a countywide contest. Since then, her passion for writing, especially poetry, has been rivaled only by her love of the 1920s and 1930s. Silent and pre-Code (1929-1934) films are a particular favorite, and she counts Clara Bow, Louise Brooks, and Jean Harlow among her muses. Her work has been featured in *Classic Images*, *Atlas Obscura*, and several other publications, as well as on the Library of Congress website. Her previous book, *Reels & Rivals: Sisters in Silent Film*, was voted one of the best film books of 2016 by Thomas Gladysz (Louise Brooks Society and *Huffington Post*).

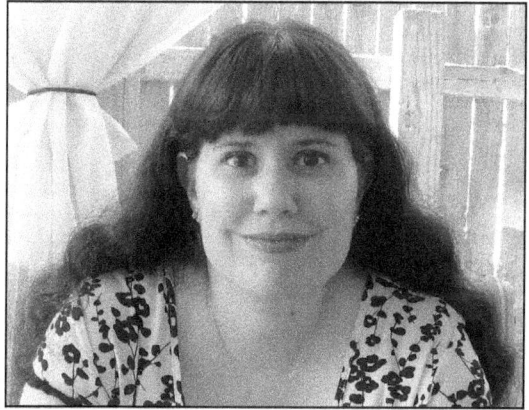

Jennifer, a vintage girl in a modern world, currently resides in her childhood home on Long Island, New York.

www.ingramcontent.com/pod-product-compliance
Lightning Source LLC
Chambersburg PA
CBHW070806100426
42742CB00012B/2267